AF651680

The Woman in the Novels of Saul Bellow

Ram Prakash Pradhan

ATLANTIC®
PUBLISHERS & DISTRIBUTORS

Published by
ATLANTIC®
PUBLISHERS & DISTRIBUTORS
B-2, Vishal Enclave, Opp. Rajouri Garden,
New Delhi-110027
Phones : 25413460, 25429987, 25466842

Sales Office
7/22, Ansari Road, Darya Ganj,
New Delhi-110002
Phones : 23273880, 23275880, 23280451
Fax : 91-11-23285873
web : www.atlanticbooks.com
e-mail : info@atlanticbooks.com

Copyright © Atlantic Publishers & Distributors, 2006

ISBN 81-269-0654-5

All rights reserved. No part of this publication may be reproduced, stored in a retrieval system, transmitted or utilized in any form or by any means, electronic, mechanical, photocopying, recording or otherwise, without the prior permission of the copyright owner. Application for such permission should be addressed to the publisher.

Printed in India
at Nice Printing Press, Delhi

Dedicated to My Parents
R.P. Pradhan
and Champa Rai

Acknowledgments

I take this opportunity to thank all those people who have directly or indirectly helped me in bringing out this book in such a nice form. I am extremely thankful to my learned Professors Dr. S.B. Shukla, Dr. A.N. Dwivedi, Dr. L.R. Sharma, Dr. S.N. Pandey, Dr. R.N. Rai, Dr. R.K. Shukla and Dr. M.S. Pandey for their constant encouragement to complete the book. I am deeply indebted to my father R.P. Pradhan, former Reader and Head, Department of English, P.G. College, Ghazipur who has been a source of academic inspiration to me. I shall be ungrateful if I do not mention of my mother Smt. Champa Rai whose motherly care and support enabled me to accomplish this task. I admire my wife Chandralekha Rai's whole-hearted cooperation, warmth, encouragement and concern ceaselessly shown in the period of writing of the present book. My two sons, Yash and Harsh, who have remained ignored and neglected during my writing work have also given me indirect incentive for it. Special thanks are to my younger brother Ravi Prakash Pradhan and his wife Tanu Rai for their valuable advice to me from time to time.

R.P. Pradhan

Preface

The book seeks to pursue major lines of enquiry about Saul Bellow's outlook towards women. The woman in his novels is neither degraded nor exalted. She stands midway according to her merit and worth. A few of women might be the mental creations of the protagonist but several of them have got real life and blood of their own. Bellow's artistic technique also imposes some kind of reservation on their free portrayal but it should not be viewed that his novels are exclusively male centred. His heroes are generally engaged in existential and transcendental problems but the female characters fail to share the same depth of emotion and intellectual problem. Hence, they are sometimes eclipsed by the central male figures. Further, we get an impression that Bellow is more interested in illustrating societal attitude towards women rather than painting their character in an individual manner. His attitude towards them is neither masochistic nor chauvinistic. His personal life may be full of a number of divorces, his novels may show frequent cases of divorces and marital disputes, cases of adultery and treachery in love but the novelist is free from any prejudice which might be born out of these factors. His outlook is universal, his canvas of woman portrait is larger. It admits all kinds of women and there is everywhere a spirit of toleration and broad outlook in their portrait.

R.P. Pradhan

Introduction

Nobel Laureate (1976) and winner of numerous awards, Saul Bellow has emerged as the most popular Jewish-American novelist in the post-war period. His novels beginning from the *Dangling Man* (1944) to *Ravelstein* (2000) are mainly the novels of male protagonists. Women with the exception of Clara Velde in *A Theft* (1989) come to play only secondary roles. They are seen mostly through the vision of their males. Some feminist critics regard Saul Bellow as a misogynist and say that he has failed to deal adequately with "femininity". It is also alleged that he is masochistic and chauvinistic in his attitude towards women. Again, he has been called a feminist and anti-feminist at the same time. Further, it is stated that his attitude towards women is not explicit as it is self-contradicting and paradoxical.

I propose to explore Bellow's technique of women's characterization and to see why Bellow does not portray them directly. I would like to study the question of Bellow's Jewish identity and to see how it affects his portrayal of women. It is also worthwhile to analyse his women in terms of Freudian psychoanalysis and to see if this restricts Bellow's portrayal of women characters. Besides, it would also be relevant to examine Bellow's personal attitude towards women and further his attempt to show the societal attitude towards them instead of drawing their character directly. Finally it would also be seen how Bellow has a preference for balance and harmony free from the state of chaos and disorder in society and how he tries to maintain a balance between feminism and anti-feminism in his portrayal of women.

Bellow's technique of women's characterization prevents him from portraying them directly. It is because the aim of Bellow is not related to the delineation of female characters in his novels. His purpose is to fight out the dominant mood of later modernist despair. He wants to oppose the cultural ideas of western civilization such as "apocalyptic romanticism, a destructive Faustian individualism, cultural elitism, existentialism, alienation ethics, absurdism, nihilism and aloofness."[1] With this end in view Bellow stands in need of having a powerful masculine voice which might be effective and dominating in the removal of general despair which is born out of such unhealthy conditions of society. Perhaps, the voice of the female protagonists would not be so expressive as that of the males. Hence, Bellow's novels are full of the vision of the male protagonists. Again, Saul Bellow wanted to introduce an entirely different male voice and set of values from Hemingwesque model "of masculinity with its hard boiled, understated existential stoicism that dominated the values and the masculine voice in American literary culture."[2] Besides, the narrators in Bellow's fictions are men who generally pass through various existential, transcendental and metaphysical problems. The female characters in the comparison of the males do not share the same depth of emotional, moral and intellectual complexities. Hence, they are eclipsed by the central male figures. This is why women occupy secondary position in his novels. They are neither degraded nor exalted. They stand midway according to their merit and worth. They are mostly perceived through the minds of the male protagonists and not directly. The male protagonists with their philosophical quest for the self and also for their discovery of the mystery of life overshadow the female characters. One cannot say that the female characters have been neglected. Bellow has presented a living picture of female characters. He has conceived them in all varieties.

The Jewish identity of Saul Bellow also affects his portrayal of women. In the Jewish religion woman has been given a place of honour in the family in the company of her husband. The old Testament which is the religious book of the Jews contains the following sermon in this regard :

> Go thy way, eat thy bread with joy, and drink thy wine with a merry heart, for God now accepteth thy works. Let thy garments be always white, and let thy head lack no

> ointment. Live joyfully with the wife whom thou lovest all the days of the life of thy vanity, which he hath given thee under the sun, all the days of thy vanity: for that is thy portion in this life, and thy labour which thou takest under the sun.[3]

The above passage shows that the Jewish religion maintains the sanctity and the integration of the family. As the nature of society is patriarchal, the woman has to occupy a subordinate place to man. There is nothing like acts of negligence and indifference towards women. In the novels of Saul Bellow there is much emphasis on the quality of integrated family. The woman has to play a vital role within the limits of the happy life of the family. Hence, priority is given to the male characters in comparison with women in his novels.

The woman of Saul Bellow may also be analysed in terms of Freudian psychoanalysis and in this respect some restrictions may be put on the portrayal of women characters. Saul Bellow is well-read in the works of Freud but he is suspicious about the role of Freudian unconscious mind which rests on the theory of determinism. Bellow does not endorse Freudian view of character determinism. However, the female characters of Bellow become the subject of psychological studies. They are not allowed their independent voice all the time. We come to learn about them through the statements of the male protagonists. It appears that a few of the female characters suffer from psychological inhibitions. Their feelings, desires and impulses appear to be hindered. Iva in *Dangling Man* cannot express herself frankly. She is victim of excessive male domination. Frances in *Henderson the Rain King* is dominated by an intellectual quality that forbids the display of emotion. Therefore, she is laconic of speech in matters of love and affection. Madeleine who pursues intellectual pursuit of mind finds it difficult to explain the importance of her academic work to her husband. Herzog himself admits that Madeleine is going through a stage of mental crisis and is "rethinking everything." She dose not love her husband but she cannot declare it openly. In this way there appears to be some amount of restraint in the character-portrayal of women from psychological point of view. Some of them are victims of repression and depression and they cannot speak out their minds frankly. They bear the psychological burden of feelings and emotions which are not let out all the time. Thus, when we analyse the female characters of Saul Bellow from the viewpoint of psychoanalysis, we find that something is left out and remains unexpressed regarding the female characters.

Saul Bellow's personal attitude towards women may also govern his vision of the woman in general. Some of the novels exhibit autobiographical sentiments. They are full of marital disputes and divorces between the protagonists and their wives. In personal life the novelist has also passed through as many as four divorces and they are likely to affect his vision of the woman to a certain extent. It is also possible that the novelist may overcome his personal prejudices, if any, and may present an objective picture of the woman through his observation and power of imagination. Bellow does not seem to assent to such adverse criticism. He has tried to convince interviewers of his high regards for his heroine Clara Velde. He informs one reporter:

> Clara Velde is a composite of all the women I have known. I had a love affair with her in the writing. I was all charged up about her. I took great satisfaction in getting close to a uniquely female intelligence—I did know a great deal about ladies.[4]

The statement shows that Bellow is as sensitive to woman as to man. Bellow in his novels advocates freedom for women. He wants them to realize their selfhood. He tries to explain their behaviour in psychological as well as sociological terms.

He is also interested in illuminating certain societal attitudes towards women rather than fully painting their character. His portrait of women is objective and free from personal bias. He maintains a balance between feminism and anti-feminism. The woman in him is not a puppet. She has got a full personality of her own. If she occupies a subordinate place to man, it is in keeping with his Jewish tradition of the family. The novelist has given us a vast and rich gallery of convincing and vivid women of all kinds. His female characters are active, alive and creative. They lead meaningful lives for themselves. They are always working, searching, struggling and growing.

Notes

1. Cronin, Gloria L., "An Introduction to Saul Bellow", *Saul Bellow Society and the Journal*—Home Page.
2. *Ibid.*
3. *The Holy Bible*, Ecclesiastes 9, ii-xviii, and 12, i-vii.
4. Chambers, Andrea. "At 73 Nobel Laureate Saul Bellow Decides He Wants to Be a Paperback Writer", *People Magazine*, 27 March 1989: 65-66, 69.

Contents

1

The Question of Jewish Identity

It has been a commonplace among the critics to raise the question of Saul Bellow's Jewish identity. His novels are full of Jewish themes, views, characters and backgrounds. However, he does not want to be labelled "an American—Jewish novelist."[1] He has always opposed what he calls the parochial pigeonholing trend. He prefers to be considered a universal writer. He states that even when he deals with specific Jewish themes, he uses them symbolic of man in general. When he received the Nobel Prize for literature in 1976, the judges of the Swedish Academy praised his "deep understanding of human nature and his fine analysis of modern culture reflected in his works, yet the Jewish themes, thought, content and background of his fiction were not mentioned."[2] No doubt, Bellow has established himself as a humanistic and conscientious novelist. There is a trait of humanism which permeates throughout his works and it gives his fiction a special quality and strength. Here, it is proposed to examine how far this humanism is linked to his Jewish themes. It is also to be seen how far Bellow's art draws upon his Jewish heritage. Is this Jewish heritage a contributory factor to his greatness as a universal writer or does it lessen the significance of his fictional work and its global character? Today, Saul Bellow has become a firmly established great American writer. The examination of the recurrent Jewish themes in his novels deserves a closer study.

A close examination of his novels shows that the Jewish themes including the quest for a Jewish identity are major ones in his works. Since the appearance of *Dangling Man* (1944) to his latest novel *Ravelstein* (2000) Jewish themes and Jewish philosophy and character inspire all his novels. They add to his greatness and do not reduce the importance of his fiction in any way. His Jewish heritage mainly functions on two levels. In the first place he chooses Jewish materials, backgrounds, situations and relationships. Secondly, he expresses the Jewish ethics, values and norms that are ingrained in his psyche and personality from his boyhood. Bellow confirms that his Judaism is indeed one of the "main foundations that I draw from in my art."[3]

Born of Russian-Jewish parents in Canada in 1915, the family of Saul Bellow moved to Chicago in 1924, and since then Bellow has entered the main stream of American culture. Although he is not regarded as an autobiographical writer, his Canadian birth along with his Jewish heritage is the backbone of his first novel *Dangling Man.* In the beginning the Jewish influence is not so pervasive as in his later novels. Bellow has been criticized by some critics for not making the plight of the Jews in Europe known to the world in this novel. Only at one point in the novel there is a reference to the Holocaust when Joseph has a nightmare. However, it may be argued that the full account of the atrocities of the Nazi Period became fully known to the world only after the end of the second world war and Bellow's novel had appeared a year earlier.

Judaism which has been a source of inspiration to the fictional writings of Saul Bellow to a certain extent comprises a set of beliefs, rituals and ethics which set the Jewish people apart from the other nations. The distinctive qualities of Judaism are its covenant with God, its humanism and its emphasis on moral action. The first Jewish philosopher was Abraham who introduced the principle of monotheism in the world. He was more concerned with establishing a relationship between God and man. In the mid-twentieth century the ethical values of Judaism were strongly attacked by Hitler and his Nazi philoscphy. Hitler stated that his war against the Jews was a war against twentieth century humanism. In 1936 in a paper read at Heidelberg University a Hitlarian Prof. of philosophy said:

> The idea of humanism...is a philosophical principle of the eighteenth century caused by conditions of that time. It is

> in no sense binding upon us as we live under different conditions and under different fate.[4]

The Holocaust which caused the mass murder of the Jews in Nazi Germany seemed to indicate to many the action of God and the reign of Nihilism. There has been plenty of Holocaust literature in Europe. Saul Bellow through his novels fought against such destructive views and he expressed a moral outlook which is an integral part of Jewish philosophy. He wanted to drive out the cloud of death that hovered over the Jewish people. He started a war against Nihilistic outlook on life. He presented a world-view which is refreshingly optimistic. Such an outlook is a product of the theory given by the Jewish philosophers. The philosophy of Judaism is a "purposeful" philosophy which is concerned not with the first cause or the origin of creation but with the meaning of creation for man. The basis of this philosophy is an ethical monotheism which is mentioned in the Bible. Such philosophy provides reason for man's existence and it stresses the human value of life. Judaism considers God as creator and man as subordinate to God. It interprets the meaning of the commandments and its application to the everyday life of the man. It establishes the moral structure of the world. Such a religion has created humanist philosophers who advocate that what appears hateful to person should not be done to his neighbour. Saul Bellow who seems to stress such moral views in his novels shows an abiding faith in the existence and purpose of human life. This spiritual outlook of Judaism is evident in his works. Bellow presents a Jewish philosophical view which takes the form of an ethical monotheism and ethical optimism in his novels. Bellow goes back to the original source which is the Bible. After Hitler's attempted obliteration of humanism, Bellow's works strive to re-establish the foundation of society in which the need for morality and the return to humanism of Judaism is expressed. Bellow has always said that the purpose of the artist is moral and therefore he makes a conscious effort at world rehabilitation. "Ethical and moral questions are at the core of his works."[5]

Dangling Man opens during the World War II with Joseph who has been a resident of Chicago for eighteen years. He is in a state of alienation and isolation. Seven months before he had been employed in the Inter American Travel Bureau but due to the war he was compelled to resign from his job and answer the army's call for induction. He is now a "dangling man" because he has quit his job to prepare for induction into the army and that induction is delayed rendering him jobless. His Jewish-Canadian citizenship is a great hurdle in his way of employment. It induces the authorities to investigate into his antecedents and delay his induction. With the result he spends his days in total boredom. The Jewish-American protagonist, Joseph, who happens to be an exile and an outcast in an alien land, has been thrown back upon himself and is unable to communicate with anybody. He is isolated from his friends. He is victim of mental depression. He rarely leaves his room and is often alone all day. Books no longer attract him. He also remains indifferent to his wife Iva. He is critical of his surroundings. He finds the world to be out of order. The world is in the terrible grip of war and Joseph sits brooding about the plight of man and finds no hope. The shadow of war is looming large over him. The loss of job makes him entirely dependent on his wife in financial matters and he does not like it. He is attracted towards another woman named Kitty. Joseph has given her a book and it becomes the cause of quarrel between Joseph and Iva. He turns to Kitty for love. Kitty advises him to seek divorce from Iva but he does not do it. Very soon he is disappointed to discover that Kitty's doors are closed for him and another lover has replaced him. He returns silently to Iva and wishes to be reconciled with her. He passes through a period of intense mental tension. He now prefers "regimentation" to freedom because for him action is redemptive. According to him the whole war is "a misfortune."[6] Joseph's agony increases when he thinks that the world has become a slaughterhouse during the war where people like his college mate Jeffersom Forman perish.

Joseph appears as a Jewish intellectual in this novel. The questions he asks of himself are related to the basic moral

Jewish philosophy: What is a man? What is the importance of human life? What is the man born for? To what extent does man control his destiny? Are we allowed to have choices? What is the meaning of true freedom? The answers to these philosophical questions reflect the general Jewish philosophy in his novel. Joseph makes a quest for "pure freedom" which might lead to the knowledge of the self and of the love. On the whole Bellow makes his hero affirm human dignity and rebel against the nihilistic attitude towards life. He makes his hero resist pessimism and speak out for humanism and such conception is related to Jewish philosophy. Joseph realizes that freedom is not possible in isolation. He makes an escape from barren freedom to the state of regimentation. He feels "perhaps the war could teach me by violence what I had been unable to learn during those months in the room."[7] The progress in the novel is from inertia to action.

Bellow's Jewish identity has found ample expression in his second novel *The Victim* (1947). The main theme of the novel is related to anti-semitism. It is worked out through the relationship between Jewish Asa Leventhal and anti-Semitic Kirby Allbee in New York. Their encounter with each other elicits the slanders of anti-Semitism which had been propagated by the Nazi government. Asa a jew who wanted to obtain a job took the help of Allbee a Gentile and secured an interview from Allbee's superior Rudiger. Rudiger was rude in his behaviour and was offended all the more by Asa's violent words and actions. There started between Rudiger and Asa a loud chaotic scene filled with recriminations. As a result of that Allbee was dismissed by Rudiger. Allbee presented himself before Asa and charged him that he had maliciously contrived the scene with Rudiger in order to avenge an anti-Semitic remark made by him earlier during the party which had been attended by Asa. Allbee further told Asa that he was responsible for the loss of his job, the separation from his wife, her death later on in an automobile accident and his present miserable condition. In this way the novel shows the struggle and conflict between the Jew and the Gentile. Apparently Asa the Jew is accused of being a victimiser by Allbee the Gentile.

However, it cannot be said clearly as to who is the victim and who is the victimiser. In this respect Keith Michael Opdahl remarks:

> But each man victimizes the other because he is a victim of himself: Jew and Gentile, victim and bigot, both men suffer from the self-persecution of imaginary fears.[8]

Asa Leventhal denied the charge as fantastic and repudiated Allbee's claim for some sort of reparation but Allbee persisted in his pursuit. Asa faced the slanderous accusations of Allbee and cried out in bitter self-defence, "Millions of us have been killed." It implied that the Jew had suffered much and it was enough to wipe out anti-Semitism. However, Asa felt that his opponent realized that the Jewish suffering was not enough. If Asa thought that anti-semitism would disappear after the Holocaust, he was mistaken. Asa was horrified by Allbee's growing anti-semitic attacks. His Jewish character asserted itself and by and by he came to acknowledge his guilt to some extent: "He liked to think [that] human meant accountable in spite of many weaknesses...."[9] Asa further examined his self and recognized essential humanity in his supposed foe. According to Clayton:

> Asa acknowledges his responsibility, offers help, and understands that Allbee is a suffering human, not merely his persecutor.[10]

Asa has an honest mind, he intends to do no evil towards Allbee, he is inspired by Jewish idealism of humanism and therefore he regards himself somewhat responsible for the misery of Allbee. The novel refers to the past history and also to the present Judeo-Christian relation. In this respect Jean Paul Sartre's remark appears to be relevant when he talks about the scapegoat theory in which the blame is shifted on the minority group like the jews whenever there is any wrong in the society and the members of this group are held responsible. Asa is ready to help Allbee out of a feeling of Jewish human solidarity but he discovers that Allbee is full of hatred towards the Jews and regards them as "interlopers" in American society. He calls the Jews "satanic forces" and Calibans who destroy the noble foundation of American society.

The Adventures of Augie March (1953) is the autobiography of a Chicago-born immigrant Jew. He has got a craving for the understanding of the mystery of life. He is a true picaresque hero in his quest for "an independent fate."[11] Augie's life begins with humiliation in the city of Chicago where he stores up all kinds of experiences joyously but later on he feels that he is surrounded by Machiavellians in the city and he gets disillusioned with them very soon. He turns inward and tries to discover his self by feeling and judging his experience. He also expresses a Jewish trait which is related to devotion towards the family. Augie March belongs to a family which is harassed by poverty and ignominy in the Chicago environment. He wants to serve his blind and weak mother and also his idiot brother. He realizes that in the city of Chicago he and his people are treated as aliens. Augie March quits the city and goes wandering round the entire American continent with his feeling of uprootedness. He has got a Jewish quest for stable home. Even at the end he remains unsettled and longs for a stable foothold. He says:

> All I want is something of my own.... I want a place of my own. If it was on Greenland's icy mountains, I'd take and go to Greenland and I'd never loan myself again to any other guy's scheme.[12]

At the end of the novel it appears that Augie fails in his ideals. His dream for a foster home and a shelter for his lonely mother and brother remains unrealized. His Jewishness is clearly evident in his concern for keeping intact the family dignity. He pawns his luxury garments in order to establish his mother respectively. Opdahl rightly remarks:

> Augie March has decided that love and home alone are a worthwhile fate but he is deprived of both by Stella's obsession with a previous lover....[13]

Augie is further dissatisfied that people at higher level try to impose a theory on him. He feels that "of all the impositions this was the worst imposition. Not just to be as they make you but to feel as they dictate."[14] Thus, the novel is a study of the ideals of Augie March and the relation of the hero to the society.

The philosophy of Judaism is part and parcel of Saul Bellow's life and it expresses itself in his writings. Bellow's consistent rejection of the category "Jewish-American writer" for himself is not a denial of his Jewishness. What he rejects is the limiting factor of categorization. Bellow freely admits his growing up in an orthodox Jewish home, he further admits that Yiddish is his first language and he has also learnt Hebrew. He states:

> At a most susceptible time of my life I was wholly Jewish. That's a gift, a piece of good fortune with which one does not quarrel.[15]

Such foundation has moulded his character, his mode of behaviour and his world-views. His ethical monotheism has become part of his overall presentation. Bellow's works are shaded by the spectre of the Holocaust, even then his belief in the hierarchical structure of the universe in which God is supreme and man has been created in the image of God remains central to his philosophical views. Bellow's characters do not speculate about the nature of God, they do not attempt to prove His existence. However, a few like Herzog express their faith in God. The heroes of Bellow are ethical individuals and therefore they cannot be separated from divinity.

> Jewishness is not only a source of guilt and worry in Bellow's novels, but also a source of strength and fullness, and in book after book, his heroes emergence from their various existential crises and their return to a healthy equilibrium—are linked with their return to their Jewish identity. This can clearly be seen in *Seize The Day* (1957) when Tommy Wilhelm discovers on his "Day of Reckoning," the eve of Yom Kippur, that the American name he adopted is the expression of his "Pretender Soul," and not his true identity. He realizes that his authentic self is epitomized by his Yiddish name, "Velvel," Little Wolf—the name his grandfather used to call him. The return of

Velvel Tommy Adler to the source of his essential Jewish identity, after experiencing the impact of a white and blue Magen David, on the wall of a Jewish death parlor, and the shock of facing the message of finitude on the face of the corpse—is the beginning of his salvation.[16]

The protagonist in Bellow's novel *Herzog* (1964) which is regarded by most critics as his masterpiece draws strength from his Jewish past in facing the problems of life. It might be taken to be an expression of Bellow's Judaism as in it man's life is viewed in terms of a contract with God. *Herzog* "is a testing of the Jewish definition of life and being, of purpose and death in the world—nothing less. It is a novel of ancient belief tested against modernism in the person of Herzog."[17] Herzog faces his ordeal of divorce with Madeleine who is his second wife. He feels that he has been a renegade from his Jewish past when he married the converted Madeleine. The hero wanders in the wilderness of despair for Madeleine whom he still loves passionately and who is haunting his mind all the time. She has left him for his best friend Valentine. Herzog is deeply shocked and he is mentally perturbed. However, he returns to his mother's grave, revives the past memories and offers Hebrew prayers. He sings aloud "How goodly are thy tents oh Jacob!" It is the triumphant cry of Moses who returns to his Jewish identity and to his people. At the end of the novel it appears that Herzog has drawn strength from his Jewish roots and he is able to overcome his guilty feelings and his obsessive passion for Madeleine. He cries out in Hebrew: "Hineni!"—"Here I am!" It is the same cry which was uttered by the Biblical Moses in the desert of Sinai when God called him out and asked him, "Moses, where are you?" Inspired by his Jewish identity Herzog is now ready to confront life again.

During the period of crisis Moses discovers that the basic principles of Christianity and Romanticism which are the foundation of twentieth century thought are really detrimental to the development of man and therefore Moses reflects, "I, a Jew...would never grasp the Christian and Faustian world idea, forever alien to me."[18] At this point he recognizes the value of his own humanistic heritage. He believes, "brotherhood makes a man human."[19] Thus, Herzog always seeks inspiration from his Jewish past and in the end he comes to achieve a state of freedom of the soul from obsession.

Herzog the learned Professor and the intellectual always struggles to preserve his Jewishness which implies a love of life and an instinct for human survival. His philosophical quest makes him brood over the loss of individuality in a collective society. As an intellectual who is an outsider even in Chicago, he feels that he is isolated from his environment. "In the service his mates had also considered him foreigner."[20] Thinking about freedom as the goal of human life Herzog feels that individuality is linked with freedom which is lost with the society when it becomes more and more politicized and organized. "This new reign of multitudes"[21] distracts him but he is hopeful that "there are human qualities still to be discovered."[22] He is concerned more with the survival of the individual and also with the survival of civilization. Jewish philosophy is rooted in the temporal world of men and man is commanded to "choose life." This philosophy is concerned by and large for living life at its fullest. According to the Bible it is indeed God's gift to man that he should eat and drink and be happy as he tolls. The struggle of Herzog is concerned with the Jewish preservation of life.

Herzog's love of family also implies his Jewish trait. Herzog has got some remembrance of his childhood how it was spent in poverty and squalor. Being the son of a bootlegger Herzog was subject to all sorts of humiliation and imaginary fear. His father an eastern European Jew and immigrant from Russia had left his country during the Revolution and had settled down to a life of abject poverty in America. Herzog has got frequent recollection of his early life:

> Napoleon street, rotten, toylike, crazy and filthy, riddled, flogged with harsh weather—the bootlegger's boys reciting ancient prayers. To this Moses' heart was attached with great power.... All he ever wanted was there. His mother did the wash, and mourned. His mother was desperate and frightened, but obstinately fighting.[23]

The environment of the street was dirty and sordid. When Herzog writes of his mother, he describes how she was a pathetic figure in this situation and how she was carrying on her struggle for existence. She was haunted by the glory of her past. Herzog inherited the characteristic of dreaming from his parents. He had nostalgic adoration for his erring father and it constitutes a Jewish trait. His sentimental fondness is expressed in these words:

> a father, a sacred being, a king. Yes, he was a king to us. My heart was suffocated by this horror. I thought I would die of it. Whom did I ever love as I loved them?[24]

Nachman his boyhood friend belongs to this phase of life as both of them were playmates on Napoleon Street at the Montreal slums. This world was also inhabited by drunkards like Nachman's uncle who wept bitterly during his drunkenness for being incapable of sending money for his wife and children in Russia. His parents stood by him in the state of their poverty and misery. Herzog feels an overwhelming pity for such miserable condition of life. The filial love and also the human love of Herzog refers to the Jewish quality in his character. Herzog's attachment with his family and his fondness for his relations may be considered as the Jewish trait in his character.

Herzog's fondness for June his daughter illustrates the traditional Jewish parental love. As he observes:

> Her face was the Herzog face, the large dark eyes his eyes, the nose his father's, Tante Zipporah's, his brother Willie's nose, and the mouth his own. Even the bit of melancholy in her beauty—that was his mother.[25]

His determination "to be same and to live and to look after the kids"[26] expresses his love for his children and his growing sense of responsibility. After returning to the Berkshires he paints the piano for June. However, Herzog is provoked to commit the murder of his "awfully good friend" Valentine Gersbach when he comes to learn that his most trusted friend is a pious fraud and he has been cuckolding him for years. He flies to Chicago with murder in his heart. He will save June but he will also prove his manhood. He takes his father's pistol from the desk and wants to shoot his friend and his wife Madeleine. Herzog is saved from committing murder by a scene which embodies Bellow's theme. He peers through the side window of Madeleine's flat and sees June in the bathtub. He watches Gersbach the man who had cuckolded him perform the father's duty. He was going to bathe Herzog's daughter:

> There were two bullets in the chamber.... But they would stay there. Herzog clearly recognized that.[27]

Herzog's decision not to murder is a perfect portrayal of Bellow's theme and this scene is the turning point in the novel. Herzog picks up June the next morning and has an auto accident and is arrested for carrying his father's gun. He had come close to violence in the conceived scene of murder and he now comes close to being a criminal but he is saved from a serious charge somehow or other. He comes to realize, "I really believe that brotherhood is what makes a man human."[28] He withdraws from the city to find peace at his countryhome. He has dedicated himself to social issues, but he enjoys also the peace of nature. At the end of the novel he seems to enjoy peace of mind. In this way Herzog expresses his Jewish character in the novel which is related to a happy family and peaceful dwelling.

Mr. Sammler's Planet (1970) is the most Jewish novel of Saul Bellow. Mr. Sammler the protagonist represents the Jewish tragedy and the Jewish uprootedness. He is a seventy-four years old Polish Jew. In the 1920s and 1930s he served in London as a correspondent of Polish papers and journals. He was also a member of a cultural circle presided over by H.G. Wells. Just prior to World War II he and his wife Antonina and their daughter Shula returned to Poland. His wife became a victim of genocidal mass murder. Rounded up by the Nazis Sammler was clubbed, he lost one eye and he was buried in a ditch with the corpse of his wife and with hundreds of others dying jews. By a miracle he escaped and found refuge in a Polish tomb. Mr. Sammler's words best describe his survival, "It was not surviving, it was only lasting.

He had lasted."[29] When the novel opens, Sammler and his daughter have been living in New York for over twenty years. Both of them have been dependent upon the physician Elya Gruner who is a nephew to Sammler and only a few years younger. It was Dr. Gruner who lifted them out of a displaced person's camp just after the war and brought them to New York. For all these years Sammler has had little to do except leading a simple life, reading extensively and observing like a philosopher.

There has been a tendency among the readers of *Mr. Sammler's Planet* to assume that the separation between the author and the protagonist is only minor. The author is a novelist and Sammler is a journalist:

> Both men are secular Jews, but Sammler has a stronger attachment to the state of Israel than Bellow has demonstrated. Both men are immigrants, but the novelist came to America as a child and was formed more by Chicago than by his Canadian childhood. Sammler, on the other hand, arrives after the second world war, which he barely survives. He is during the novel's present, in his seventies, a prime specimen of what used to be called the "good European," a man shaped by the internationalist culture of upper-class Polish Jews.[30]

This dispossessed Jew who is haunted by the memories of Holocaust asserts his faith and also his destiny with his race and with mankind. His visit to Israel as a correspondent during the six days war and also his previous visit to Jerusalem speak of his faith in his race. He is an intellectual Jew who is familiar with the philosopher Schopenhauer though he knows that the philosopher did not care for the Jews. All these things emphasize his quest for the root—a sense of belonging with his race. Even at the age of seventy-two he cannot stay away from the war which is causing the extermination of the Jewish race in Israel, he gives a vivid description of the dead bodies lying exposed in the sun and getting decomposed gradually. Mr. Sammler presents the picture of the war as the correspondent:

> The odor was like damp cardboard. The clothes of the dead, greenish-brown sweaters, tunics, shirts were strained by the swelling, the gases, the fluids. Swollen gigantic arms, legs, roasted in the sun. The dogs ate human roast.[31]

The purpose of mentioning this is to stress Mr. Sammler's Jewish experience, his involvement in the war and his sense of victimization as a Jew. Having gone through the trauma of war, Mr. Sammler observes the whole thing in an ironical manner, "It was a real war. Everyone respected killing. Why not the priest?"[32] It is clear that Sammler's sympathy for his race is great and he cannot excuse the anti-semitism of the Germans or similar irrational attitude of intolerance expressed by other nations. Mr. Sammler always lays emphasis on the fact of being an oriental and a jew. Instinctively he recognizes a close bond with the Indians with their similar situations:

> I seem to be a depth man rather than a height man. I do not personally care for the illimitable. The ocean, however deep, has a top and bottom, whereas there is no sky ceiling.[33]

After his association with Dr. Govind Lal he develops mystical feelings and seems to endorse Buddhist conception of Nirvan through the consciousness of such symbols as "red flush," "vast crimson envelope" and "a sky filling silk fabric." The strain of Orientalism is expressed in his idea of other worldliness and in his craving for freedom from the "bondage of the ordinary and the finite."[34]

Sammler's love for his kith and kin particularly Dr. Gruner his dying nephew, his daughter Shula and the young people speaks of his Jewish sense of family. If an analysis of his relation with these people is made, one comes to discover his love of humanity and his feeling of filial love. This concern for his family is a Jewish quality which expresses itself through love, personal relationship, selflessness and charity. Mr. Sammler has got unreserved admiration for Dr. Elya Gruner who is known for his love of humanity. Dr. Gruner is a real gentleman, he has earned a lot of wealth but he remains incorruptible. Besides, he has got "on the whole kindly...and a lot of family feeling."[35] Dr. Gruner remains an immigrant in heart and seeks his roots and relations with the Jewish people. It is he who has saved Mr. Sammler and his daughter from the refugee camps and has provided them the means to live comfortably. Dr. Gruner's love for Israel is strongly embedded in his personality:

> He has been buying Israel bonds and real estate, gave away heavily embossed silver ball-point pens, made in Israel, had a passion for kinship.[36]

Even while lying in hospital he remembers his Jewish relations. Sammler is impressed by the human heartedness of Dr. Gruner. Even Sammler's humanity rises above narrow feelings as he ignores the defects of Dr. Gruner. Sammler admits in his heart that Gruner's defects are superficial and they have not affected his natural sensibility. Mr. Sammler is harassed by the possibility of Dr. Gruner's imminent death. He expects that his children Angela and Wallace Gruner shall be equally upset for their dying father. In fact, he comes to discover that the Jewish idea of family and community is disintegrating. He also observes that the children of Dr. Gruner are concerned more with their sexual affairs and are careless for filial love. He blames Dr. Gruner for providing the children with wealth and luxury which makes them poorer in matters of heart.

Mr. Sammler leads death-in-life existence in alien surroundings, death has been no stranger to him, however, he mourns the death of Dr. Gruner with genuine emotion. He is amazed to find that Dr. Gruner has made his peace with death. Mr. Sammler knows well that the shadow of death looms large on human being in general, he becomes more conscious of the virtue of human relationship and compassion in the person who is departing from the world. In that way he pays the highest tribute to the humanitarian outlook of Dr. Gruner.

Mr. Sammler goes to Israel to defend his daughter Shula from the torture of her cruel husband Eisen. However, he cannot forgive her act of stealing the Indian Scientist's manuscript and her attempt at avoiding the charge of theft.

He is angry at her "theft of intellectual property."[37] He cannot exonerate his own daughter because in his opinion Shula's stealing is an act of contemporary lawlessness.

> Other people may make new rules as they go along but I will not, and you will not put me in that position.[38]

It shows that he firmly upholds the cause of truth which is related to Judaism.

The love of Mr. Sammler to his own planet which is the earth is expressive of his Jewish ideal. Mr. Sammler does not like the idea of exodus from the earth and going to the moon for habitation as has been given by the Indian Scientist. He wants to make this planet habitable through order, love and bond of human relationship. He cannot make a compromise with evil in the person of the Negro pickpocket who was vulgar enough to show him his penis. However, he pities the Negro pickpocket for his vulgarity and act of stealing. It reveals his undying humanitarian impulse. In his opinion the urban life in the heart of New York has manifested the force of disintegration and has gone out of order. His attitude is typically Jewish and it shows the Jewish identity of Saul Bellow.

Critics such as Liela Goldman, Allan Chavkin and Herbert J. Smith variously affirm that *Humboldt's Gift* (1975) is a Jewish novel. Other critics advance different views and they suggest that *Humboldt's Gift* is a novel of Schopenhauerian pessimism. There might be ideological differences in judging the character of the novel but on the whole the novel seems to express Jewish way of life. Humboldt Fleisher the son of Jewish Hungarian immigrants rises to great literary eminence by virtue of his "Harleguin Ballads" at the age of twenty-two. He becomes a great writer of 1930s. He is able to attract Charles Citrine, a student of the university of Wisconsin who undertakes a trip of fifty hours with borrowed money in order to have a glimpse of the famous writer Von Humboldt Fleisher. Their friendship develops day by day and turns Charles Citrine into a protege of Humboldt. Charles Citrine becomes the successor of Humboldt as Humboldt sinks into oblivion within his rise of ten years. It is through the reminiscences of Charles Citrine that one comes to learn the "turbid ebb and flow" of Humboldt's life. Through the ballads of Humboldt, one comes to learn about his Jewish-Hungarian immigrant father who was leading a life of luxury in Chicago and who fell a victim to mental depression due to his sudden loss of fortune and it caused the failure of his heart. Citrine remembers how Humboldt suffered from insomnia but even then he became learned while reading Marx, Toynbee and Freud. However, more than anything else he had got a passion for modern poetry. "His real worth was literary."[39]

It is learnt through *Humboldt's Gift* that the Germans wanted to honour Humboldt's poetry by inviting him to lecture in Germany and the Free University of Berlin but Humboldt refused to go there. He explained to the Jewish protagonist Charles Citrine that such a visit "would have reminded him of the Holocaust every single minute of his time there."[40] Humboldt and Charles Citrine, the double protagonists in the novel are always conscious of the shadow of the persecution of the Jews under the Germans. Both of them are creative artists in the mechanical world of America which has no sympathy for such people who pursue literature. It is because this is the age of technology and science:

> May be America didn't need art and inner miracles. It had so many outer ones. The U.S.A. was a big operation, very big. The more it, the less we.[41]

The tragedy of the two writers is born out of the fact that one of them is dead and the other is on the brink of disgrace. The living one is bringing the dead back to life by his reminiscences. The novelist makes a search for the real meaning of life through the study of these two figures. The artist is an intellectual and a Jew and is concerned with the life of the mind and the spirit. The intellectual and the aesthete who also happen to be two poets pass a hard life in an alien atmosphere. They are visionary, intellectual, sensual, metaphysical, spiritual and above all Jewish. The poet makes a quest for identity in a world of science and technology. The spiritual quest which is related to the immortality of the soul becomes a constant preoccupation with Citrine. The novelist shows how Humboldt the visionary suffers the fate of an idealist and a dreamer and his visions become meaningless. Humboldt in the twentieth century America continued his quest both for poetry and power and was out to create a myth but he met failure and frustration:

> He wanted to be magically and cosmically expressive and articulate, able to say anything, he wanted also to be wise, philosophical, to find the common ground of poetry and science.[42]

On the other hand Charles Citrine reached the pinnacle of glory and Kennedy invited him to the White House. His play "Von Trenck" continued to be staged at the theatre for eight months while Humboldt was spreading calumny against him. He avenged himself by drawing six thousand seven hundred and sixty-three dollars and fifty cents from Charles Citrine's account in the bank. They had signed the blank cheque in each others name as a sign of their friendship and Humboldt committed an act of inhuman betrayal. There was complete estrangement between the two and Citrine was no longer a loyal friend of Humboldt.

As the title of the novel shows, the gift of Humboldt comes to Citrine after his death and resurrects him from a state of disgrace and misery. This is the triumph of the visionary who works out a miracle through the efficacy of his art and in that way he brings about the victory of the writers and the artists in a scientific society which seems to have made them an obsolete class of people. The process of revival starts soon after the death of Humboldt. Charles Citrine is in his mid-fifties when Humboldt has been dead for five or six years ago. He starts thinking about the poet's power during his European tour:

> A poet is what he is in himself because a voice sounds in his soul which has a power equal to the power of societies, states and regimes.[43]

According to him "art and truth" are as permanent as the poem "Grecian Urn" of John Keats. In that way Humboldt bestows a valuable gift on Citrine. Citrine becomes the successor of Humboldt and he has to carry on his unfinished work which is related to the power of the artist. Citrine now remembers his old comrade with love and affection and attracts the people towards him who have got academic interest. He is haunted by the memories of his friend and repents of his own callousness towards him during the last days of his life. He becomes more and more aware of an eternal bond with him. The novel is a victory of spirit over sheer material existence and it also pays attention to the immortality of the soul. This theme makes a progress on the earlier novels of Saul Bellow. *Humboldt's Gift* concentrates on the issue of death and the immortality of the spirit.

Citrine acquits Humboldt of the charge of betrayal and starts thinking about his greatness—"Humboldt became one of my significant dead."[44] Citrine's meditation on "the significant dead" assumes spiritual importance for the man who is worried about the problem of human existence. He feels that he must meet Humboldt, his parents and his dead mistress in the other world after his death. He is inspired by his pursuit of "the knowledge of the higher world and its attainments."[45] He comes to cherish the idea that human soul is valuable and it is indestructible. He is able to understand Humboldt's insomnia in his own way and thinks that his friend could not sleep because being a poet he found the materialism of the world very suffocating. Death does not appear to him an object of distress as it had appeared for Henderson, Leventhal, Tommy and Mr. Sammler. He contemplates about life after death and makes a quest for truth and for the meaning of death. In this way the metaphysical problem of life and death is closely related to Jewish philosophy.

Saul Bellow is an international literary figure who handles the issues of world-wide interest and beneath such theme there lies the fundamental quality of humanism which is an integral part of Jewish philosophy. Judaism has provided his fictions rich materials which are related to human condition and the progress of civilization. These factors are contributory to his greatness as the writer of fiction.

Saul Bellow like a humanist is haunted again and again by the ugly events of the Second World War which caused devastation of life and society. The protagonists of Bellow's novels want to recreate the bond of humanitarianism through their use of such words as "good," "humanity," "dignity" and "responsibility." These words have evolved into European Jewish culture and they comprise much of the ethical optimism of Judaism. Nazism which was opposed to the Jewish philosophy of humanism sought to eradicate the ethics of humanism along with the intended extinction of the Jewish people. Bellow's characters seek to establish the ideal of humanism. A Jewish child's first commandment from his parents is, "Be an ethical caring human being." Bellow's heroes make a search for the answer to the question, "How should a good man live?" The heroes of his novels are not all good. They may be flawed individuals but they try to improve their condition in the course of their lives and such attempt makes them human and joins them with the human struggle for survival. In this way the Jewish theme contributes to the broad conception of his novels.

An understanding of the philosophy of Judaism indicates that Bellow's perspective is Jewish. "Bellow writes in the manner of an Old Testament prophet, for Bellow is essentially a religious person"[46] and literature for him "is a way of coming closure to God."[47]

We can clearly discern from the above examination that Bellow's outlook is essentially humanistic and optimistic and it is linked to his Jewish roots and "his art to a great extent draws upon his Jewish heritage."[48]

Notes

1. Aharoni, Ada. The Jewish Themes in the Works of Nobel Prize: Saul Bellow *Thirteenth World Congress of Jewish Studies, Jerusalem,* 12 June 2002.
2. *Ibid.*
3. *Ibid.*
4. Quoted in **Max Weinreich**, *Hitler's Professors*, New York: Yivo, 1946, 21.

5. Kakutani, Michiko. "A Talk with Saul Bellow: On His work and Himself", *The New York Times Book Review,* 13 December 1981, 28-31.
6. *Dangling Man,* Penguin Books, 1987, 52. (All subsequent citations from this novel refer to this text).
7. *Dangling Man,* 158.
8. Opdahl, Keith Michael. *The Novels of Saul Bellow: An Introduction,* University Park and London, The Pennsylvania State University Press, 1967, 56.
9. *The Victim,* Penguin Books, 1947, 154 (All subsequent citations from this novel refer to this text).
10. Clayton, John Jacob. *Saul Bellow: In Defense of Man* (second edition), Indiana University Press, 1979, 142.
11. *The Adventures of Augie March,* New York: Viking Press, 1953, 401 (All subsequent citations from this novel refer to this text).
12. *The Adventures of Augie March,* 526.
13. Opdahl, 93.
14. *The Adventures of Augie March,* 417.
15. Kulshrestha, Chirantan. "A Conversation with Saul Bellow," *Chicago Review*, 23, No. 1, 7-15.
16. Aharoni, Ada. The Jewish Themes In the Works of Nobel Prize: Saul Bellow *Thirteenth World Congress of Jewish Studies, Jerusalem,* 12 June 2002.
17. Bernstein, Melvin. "Jewishness, Judaism and the American Jewish Novel" *Chicago Jewish Forum* 23 (1965): 281.
18. *Herzog*, Penguin Books, 1976, 235 (All subsequent citations from this novel refer to this text).
19. *Herzog*, 272.
20. *Ibid.*, 170.
21. *Ibid.*, 163.
22. *Ibid.*
23. *Ibid.*, 140.
24. *Ibid.*, 147.
25. *Ibid.*, 256.
26. *Ibid.*, 27.
27. *Ibid.*, 257.
28. *Ibid.*, 272.
29. *Mr. Sammler's Planet,* 75.

30. Guttmann, Allen. "Saul Bellow's Mr. Sammler" *Contemporary Literature* 14.2 (1973).
31. *Mr. Sammler's Planet*, 250.
32. *Ibid.*, 202.
33. *Ibid.*, 147.
34. *Ibid.*, 95.
35. *Ibid.*, 62.
36. *Ibid.*, 67.
37. *Ibid.*, 154.
38. *Ibid.*
39. *Humboldt's Gift*, 7.
40. Aharoni, Ada. The Jewish Themes in the Works of Nobel Prize: Saul Bellow *Thirteenth World Congress of Jewish Studies, Jerusalem*, 12 June 2002,
41. *Humboldt's Gift*, 9.
42. *Ibid.*, 119.
43. *Ibid.*, 304.
44. *Ibid.*, 12.
45. *Ibid.*, 110.
46. Goldman, L.H. "Saul Bellow and the Philosophy of Judaism," *Studies in Literary Imagination* 17, No. 2 (1984): 81-95.
47. Lamont, Rosette. *Bellow Observed,* Mosaic 8, No. 1 (Fall 1974), 256.
48. Aharoni, Ada. The Jewish Themes in the Works of Nobel Prize: Saul Bellow *Thirteenth World Congress of Jewish Studies, Jerusalem*, 12 June 2002.

Men and Women in the Novels

2

More than any other American novelist of the Post-War period, Saul Bellow has explored thoroughly the effects of American cultural anxiety through a variety of characters. His men and women are out to fight against the psychological maladies of modernist despair, alienation ethics, cultural elitism, existentialism, absurdism, nihilism and destructive Faustian individualism. Through his people Saul Bellow vehemently opposes the attitudes of defeated wastelanders who appear in contemporary American fiction and who lament the failure of society and the human experience. In an age of technology and rationalism, Bellow seems to affirm Judeo-Christian religious and social values through his characters. A study of Bellow's men and women is imperative in order to understand the spirit of society and the human nature portrayed in the novels.

Some critics are of the opinion that Bellow's novels express American masculine views through the male protagonists and women characters occupy only secondary position and very few of them are given free voice:

> While feminist critics might well hold Bellow responsible for failing to create fully-imagined women, he makes no bones about the fact that he is primarily interested in men, and particularly in the "man" of poetic sensibility and mantic awareness. In fact, much of Bellow's brilliant comedy erupts from the narcissistic nature of these male characters whom Bellow both loves and chastises for their shortcomings.[1]

All his heroes are adult males. Only two women Hattie in *The Yellow House* and Clara Velde in *A Theft* function as central protagonists. The majority of the novels have been written in the first person in the form of monologues. They throw light on the inner life and the mental condition of the male heroes. However, Bellow's novels are never written about any one person. What they do is to explore a particular human condition through the characters. Bellow's protagonist is invariably an everyman.

The study of men and women in the novels of Saul Bellow presents a certain vision of life which has been lived at different levels under different conditions. The protagonists of Bellow's novels are often discovered in a state of self-conflict but they are also confronted in their conflict with the society in which they live. The main concern of the novelist is to show the plight of man in a society which appears to be hostile to the achievement of their ideals. In novels like *Dangling Man* (1944), *The Victim* (1947), *Seize The Day* (1956), and *Herzog* (1964), the protagonists make a struggle against the callous forces of society and also indulge in the examination of their inner self. The quest of the heroes in these novels is more internal and meditative. Again, there is another class of novels in which the journey is external and world-wide and the hero comes to learn the meaning of life through his direct confrontation with the forces of evil. *The Adventures of Augie March* (1953) has got a picaresque mode of narration and the protagonist makes a journey to Mexico and Europe. *Henderson The Rain King* (1959) takes the protagonist to the interior of Africa. In *Humboldt's Gift* (1975) there is the wide tour of Europe and in *Mr. Sammler's Planet* (1970) the hero goes to Israel. In *The Dean's December* (1982) there is journey to Communist Rumania which is the country of Eastern Europe. In all these countries the hero is made to study human life beyond the borders of Chicago and New York and in that way the hero comes to learn a variety of cultures. In *The Dean's December* the hero studies the contrasting political and economic systems of a communist country and he examines the relative merits of life in Chicago and New York and also the life lived at Rumania. He finds out that life in the communist country is a closed life under iron curtain and regimentation but life in American cities of New York and Chicago is also full of inhuman crimes. The protagonists of Bellow enjoy a broader vision of life. They communicate with the East through the study of esoteric philosophy and discussion with people like Dr. Govind Lal who is an Indian scientist. In the end the protagonists of Bellow return from Mexico, Africa, Spain and Rumania to their original places. Their physical journey enables them to see different stages of life in the external world but they also probe deep into their souls and brood over the themes of death, immortality of soul and omnipotence of God. The heroes are not flat characters, they show improvement in their discovery of life. The heroes of Bellow move away from western materialism to a metaphysical aspect of life. They make a certain progression, a certain determination to overcome the forces of despair, a certain reconciliation to the problems of life. There seems to be a spirit of development in the heroes from inaction to action, from existential fear to mystical insight, from materialism to platonic idealism. In later novels there is an assertion of the immortality of soul and also a faith in rebirth which is an eastern attitude. It may be observed that novelist's affirmation of God's omnipotence is a blend of the American transcendentalism, Jewish faith and Eastern mysticism.

In *Dangling Man* the protagonist Joseph is alienated from himself and his environment. Having resigned his job to answer the army's call for induction, he has to wait for a long time. During the period of leisure, "the Dangling Man" Joseph makes a philosophical quest which takes the form of several enquiries into the nature of human life. He says, "I must know what I myself am."[2] Living alone in his room for ten hours a day Joseph attempts to follow the advice of Diderot-Moi "to shut oneself up in a garret, eat a dry crust, drink plain water and try to find oneself." After the advice of Moi the search of Joseph narrows from common humanity to the knowledge of his ownself. Joseph emerges as a self-indulgent man, he eats too much, quits writing, sleeps late, gains weight and sinks as he himself recognizes into Hobbes's "nasty, brutish and short" realities of purposeless existence. He deteriorates into a state of anti-hero, he separates himself from the cycle of nature and the cycle of human life. He lives in a vacuum. He has always been aloof from the seasonal changes. Christmas is spoiled by his selfishness, New Year's Eve goes without enjoyment. Even his sixth wedding anniversary goes awry marked by gloomy atmosphere. He places inordinate value on his own freedom and individuality. He is indifferent towards his wife Iva but accepts her sacrifice gladly. He depends on her financial support. For the time being he is also separated from his wife and turns to another lady Kitty for love but very soon he is disillusioned to discover that Kitty is loving another man and cannot pay attention to him. At the end of his spiritual journey which has been made for the knowledge of the self and also for "pure freedom," Joseph comes to realize that he cannot be free except in giving himself away:

> We struggle perpetually to free ourselves. Or, to put it somewhat differently, while we seem so intently and even desperately to be holding on to ourselves, we would far rather give ourselves away. We do not know how. So, at times, we throw ourselves away. When what we really want is to stop living so exclusively and vainly for our own sake, impure and unknowing, turning inward and self-fastened.[3]

Therefore, he prefers a life in the army to a life of solitary confinement to the room of an individual. He realizes:

> Goodness is achieved not in a vacuum, but in the company of other men, attended by love. I, in this room, separate, alienated, distrustful, find in my purpose not an open world, but a closed, hopeless jail. My perspectives end in the walls.[4]

Joseph achieves another important realization that his quest is the common human quest:

> We are all drawn towards the same craters of the spirit—to know what we are and what we are for, to know our purpose, to seek grace.[5]

He recognizes that his destiny is also the common human destiny, his spirit tells him, "Everybody else is dangling too."[6] Joseph joins the human race once again and he is no longer cut off from the spring of life. He is reborn in the spring of the year, he celebrates the first day of spring by walking in the park. He further realizes that celebrating life means accepting death. He urgently requests his draft board to call him into selective service. Through his wide meditation Joseph is led to think that instead of making philosophical preparation to live he must prepare himself to die. Death is the great fact of life. Death is ever present in the unconscious thought of Joseph. He feels that his landlady's death is an ideal example. After passing a life of service to others, she died surrounded by her loving family and friends. As her life has meant something, her death has also a sense of grandeur. Thus, there is a development of human quality in the life of Joseph from the fallen state of stagnation and anti-heroism.

Bellow's heroes like Joseph, Asa Leventhal, Tommy Wilhelm and Herzog are often troubled by the discovery of their true self. The problems of the self are various, internal as well as external, physical as well as metaphysical, historical as well as transcendental. The question arises about the real nature of the self which is pursued by the protagonists. Is it static or is it ever in a state of flux? Bellow himself is regarded as the advocate of the self and an abominator of society. Some critics have described him just the reverse of this view and take him to be the rejector of the self and an affirmer of society. However, a "strong sense of self" seems to be the greatest concern of Bellow and his protagonists. It may be argued that the claims of the self and society are not inimical to each other. The person who has been able to discover his true self may enjoy a state of serenity and may accept the society in which he lives. Even if he is detached from society, he may not be hostile to it. The protagonists of Saul Bellow make an attempt to realize their true self. They may feel uncomfortable in society but in the end they try to study its mystery and return to it. They also express from time to time that the same self is capable of doing stupid things and it may indulge in romantic nonsense. Bellow himself refers to this duality in *Distractions of a Fiction Writer*:

> There is a man's own greatness,
> and then there is the greatness of
> his imbecility—both are eternal.[7]

Bellow's pursuit of the human soul may be studied in the central consciousness of his characters. In his earlier works the desire of the spirit for transcending physical world and death is incipient but in his later works like *Herzog, Mr. Sammler's Planet* and *The Dean's December* the quest becomes more serious. The heroes of Bellow are philosophical and they raise fundamental questions about the reality of life. They try to find out if there is anything stable in life. Their search is born out of their struggle with their circumstances. They live in a world of distraction and frustration. They are ridden by anxiety, guilt, mental tensions, boredom and fear of death. They feel crushed by the bitter facts of life. They drift aimlessly in a world which appears to them meaningless. They are exposed to various kinds of strong winds from all sides. Therefore, they try to peep into their true self. They come to regard the true self as something essential and real. They also come to realize that it "is given rather than invented."[8]

All the heroes of Bellow are engaged in the exploration of reality. They take it for granted that the true self is a seeker of reality about human existence and also about the nature of the world. There are some heroes like Joseph, Leventhal and Wilhelm who withdraw from the world and try to discover reality in their inner self. There are others like Augie and Henderson who make their quest external. The later heroes like Herzog, Sammler, Corde and Citrine are meditative and try to experience "the mystical great things of life."[9]

Opdahl rightly remarks:

> Each of Bellow's heroes find the climax of his story—and a sense of great revelation—in confrontation with death. Joseph's final walk in the Alley is associated with the ancient figure of his dreams, and his subsequent request for induction—itself a confrontation of death—brings relief. Leventhal awakes to find his life in danger, Allbee about to die, and, at the end of their struggle, a sense of completion. Augie too undergoes such experience in his fight with Basteshaw in the lifeboat and his violent breakup with Thea, Wilhelm breaks down before a corpse and Henderson witnesses Dahfu's death. In each case the

hero vacillates before a threat or ordeal and then confronts the source of that threat in the death scene. In each there is a pattern of resistance, embrace and release reminiscent of Leventhal's description of the swinging door.[10]

Bellow has often stressed that reality cannot be discovered through rationality. He further affirms that external reality is not true reality. He even suspects whether the physical world is real at all. Joseph feels that "the real world is not here at all and what is at hand is spurious and copied."[11] Herzog believes:

> We have ground to hope that a life is something more than a cloud of particles, mere facticity. Go through what is comprehensible and you conclude that only the incomprehensible gives any light.[12]

The heroes of Bellow go beyond physical reality to be able to discover spiritual reality. They want to reach this stage through intuitive experience. The novelist puts emphasis on those critical moments of the life of the hero when he "transcending the immediate pressure of his environment and the limiting conditions of his social matrix, asks himself some fundamental question about the nature of his humanity."[13]

Bellow's transcendental vision has become religious by and by. "The problem and goal of all of Bellow's heroes is religious transcendence."[14] Opdahl calls it "problem" because it is born out of the religious aspirations of the heroes and he considers it to be a goal because "only transcendence will finally answer the problems they face."[15] The early heroes of Bellow may be slow about the revelation of a religious kind of temper but the later ones like Herzog, Sammler, Citrine and Corde are much more inclined towards the affirmation of religious transcendence. Sammler in the concluding lines of the novel expresses that each individual has an "intensive awareness of transcendent reality."[16] Similarly Citrine is also aware of the mystery of life. He makes a distinction between the knowledge of mind and the understanding of the soul. He observes:

> The old philosophy distinguished between knowledge achieved by effort (ratio) and knowledge received

> (intellectus) by the listening a soul that can hear the essence of things and comes to understand the marvellous.[17]

Bellow is rather in agreement with Kierkegaad who affirms the existence of soul, he does not endorse the view of Sartre who denies its existence.

Herzog is the first protagonist of Bellow who undergoes the process of self-examination in a conscious manner. He is really in his mind at the outset of the novel. He turns inward for his mental sustenance. In the opening sentence of the novel Herzog says, "If I am out of my mind, it's all right with me, thought Moses Herzog."[18] However, "Herzog's mind is the setting for the action, much of it backward moving."[19] Whether in his mind or whether in his statement that he is out of mind, Herzog is a regular thinker and an intellectual:

> Resuming his self-examination, he admitted that he had been a bad husband—twice. Daisy, his first wife, he had treated miserably. Madeleine, his second had tried to do him in. To his son and his daughter he was a loving but bad father. To his own parents he had been an ungrateful child. To his country, an indifferent citizen. To his brothers and his sister, affectionate but remote. With his friends, an egotist. With love, lazy. With brightness, dull. With power, passive. With his own soul, evasive.[20]

The chain of his thought is going on in a ceaseless manner. He is filled with a sense of remorse in what he has done with his first wife Daisy and his second wife Madeleine. He admits that he has been a bad husband, a bad father and an ungrateful child. He has also been an indifferent citizen to his country. These are the reflections of Herzog about his own self.

In his novel *Herzog* Bellow speculates upon the relevance of romanticism to modern life. It is this particular concern that determines the character of the novel. Can Herzog prevail as a romantic humanist in a world that has grown increasingly brutal and immoral? Herzog is continuing his studies in romanticism. He feels that it is a world of wastelanders who dislike his romanticism and his idealism. Their brutal "realism" makes a mockery of his idealism. Herzog would like to eliminate the Utopian tendency of some of the early romantics like Rousseau who start with the assumption that man is essentially good. Herzog wants to abandon the visionary aspects of the romanticism of the early 19th century. He realizes that the romantics must be tough-minded in a cynical modern world. He agrees to Hulme's attack on romanticism in which man's innate goodness has been called in question. Hulme follows the Bible in which man is an original sinner. An original sinner cannot be fundamentally good hence the idea of Rousseau is opposed to the idea of the Bible or the idea of Hulme in which man is originally a sinner. In describing man as essentially good, the romantics lessened the subordination of simple man to God and they affirmed the individuality of man. Although Bellow would not go so far as to see man as a god, he does believe, as Wordsworth exclaims, that only on earth can man find joy and harmony.

The portrayal of life in the novels of Saul Bellow may not be presented in chronological order because his novels do not show successive improvement upon each other. They seem to form an independent unit. The early novels like *Dangling Man, The Victim* and *Seize The Day* are often arranged as the victim group of novels. They deal with the depressive theme of a lonely man who has been entrapped in a difficult situation. However, the order is broken because the novel *The Adventures of Augie March* precedes *Seize The Day* and it deals with a picaresque type of theme with its innumerable episodes which make an atmosphere of sunshine and joy. Again, some novels deal with the theme of the inner world of mind and spirit and they cannot be studied in successive order. Among such philosophical novels mention may be made of *Dangling Man, The Victim, Seize The Day* and *Herzog* because their protagonists like Joseph, Asa Leventhal, Tommy Wilhelm and Herzog follow the discovery of the true nature of their souls. Further, some novels like *Dangling Man, The Adventures of Augie March* and *Herzog* have got Chicago as their primary locale and others like *The Victim, Seize The Day* and *Mr. Sammler's Planet* are related to the city of New York.

Frank D. McConnell remarks about the significance of the two cities in Bellow's novels:

> He was raised in Chicago and now lives there as a member of the University of Chicago committee on social thought while his residence in New York was mainly during the years which produced his grimmest books and may well have been a somber period in his own life.[21]

In *Humboldt's Gift* Chicago and New York both the cities figure prominently while in *The Dean's December* the action is related to Chicago and Bucharest. Besides, *Henderson The Rain King* is set in New England and Africa. There is a regular alternation of locale in his novels. Hence, the novels may be studied in an independent manner for discovering the life of the period.

Seize The Day forms a special class of study because it has got a classical neatness of plot. It is highly artistic as it is the study of a single day in the life of its protagonist Tommy Wilhelm. The novel describes the failure and the drowning of the hero. Tommy Wilhelm has foolishly quit his job and has no money to meet the demand of his wife. His relations with his elderly father whom he has denied by changing his name have come to a breaking point. He has lost his identity and he is known simply as Dr. Adler's son. He keeps up the pretence of a successful man but his life has been a series of blunders and failures. All his decisions have come to nothing:

> He had decided that it would be a bad mistake to go to Hollywood and then he went. He had made up his mind not to marry his wife, but ran off and got married.[22]

As a young man he intended to become a film star for making a quick success in his life. He left his studies to the utter disapproval of his parents. The film test flopped and instead of entering the world of Hollywood he had to choose menial jobs for maintaining his life. His marriage was also unhappy as his wife troubled him by draining money out of him constantly. He was also separated from his sons whom he loved very much. He was disappointed with the members of his family and he adopted the role of a hypocrite in order to conceal his real self. At the age of forty-three he was exhausted and broken. Spurned by his father, persecuted by his wife, he was also victimised by a trickster. He felt that he was living in the world of Machiavellians. He was desperately isolated and profoundly alone. He realized that he was living in a state of society in which Mammon or God of Wealth was all in all. He lived at the hotel Gloriana in the city of New York where in his opinion there was no compassion, no understanding and no love. His father a retired physician in his 80s also lived there. The son wanted to seek out the protection of his father in the long run. He needed money and his father could easily supply but he did not give him anything. The appeal of Tommy to his father is always futile. His father's response is always cold, bitter and angry. He is conscious of his son's past failures and present ignominy. More than money Tommy needs communication with an understanding of heart. Again and again, he appeals to his father for compassion but he cannot elicit any sympathy from him. On meeting rebuff and humiliation from the side of his father Tommy turns to Dr. Tamkin for help. He falls a prey to Tamkin's sinister motives and shrewdness and in this way he undergoes a stage of deep suffering. He is mentally and morally tortured. He is haunted by the need of money for his bare sustenance. He thinks:

> There's money everywhere. Everyone is shoveling it in.... But oh, if I could only work out a little steady income from this.[23]

Tamkin tells him that "money-making" is a murderous social activity:

> Money-making is aggression. That's the whole thing. The functionalistic explanation is the only one. People come to the market to kill...only they haven't got the genuine courage to kill, and they erect a symbol of it. The money.[24]

Tamkin who has proved a cheat to him makes him realize certain truths about human life. He may not live up to his moral values but he prepares Wilhelm for his spiritual regeneration. It is the irony of situation that the degraded man

Tamkin further teaches him the difference between the true soul and false soul:

> In here, the human bosom-mine, your's everybody's-there isn't just one soul. There's a lot of souls. But there are two main ones, the real soul and a pretender soul.[25]

Tommy Wilhelm is a victim hero. He is "like the other heroes, a victim of society."[26] However, he is more a victim of himself than of society. He knows that he is going to commit mistake in doing something yet he does it. He goes on repeating mistake after mistake.

Wilhelm's drowning is the climax of his day of failure. The description of this tragic event is symbolical. The water in which he drowns is both the world and his masochistic self. They have come to murder him. If the water pours into Wilhelm from the outside, it also wells up from within. Throughout the day of Wilhelm Bellow writes, "he smelled the salt odor of tears in his nose."[27] When Wilhelm loses everything on the market "his unshed tears rose and rose and he looked like a man about to drown."[28] "Wilhelm drowns in his own tears."[29] The novel suggests a note of joy in the drowning of Wilhelm. It calls it the "ultimate need" which is consummated. It is the transcendence of sorrow which shows that there is a greater reality beyond the limit of the physical world. Wilhelm found "the ultimate need" of his heart. Bellow hints at the hero's progress from destruction to redemption. The hero welcomes sorrow and in that way he welcomes his own identity. The hero in the past remembered some lines from Keats's *Endymion:*

> Come then, sorrow!/ .../ I thought to leave thee/ And deceive thee/ But now of all the world I love thee best.[30]

In the early criticism *Seize The Day* was regarded as a typical modernist alienation literature but in modern time the novel is taken to represent a stage of transition from the dark traditions of modernism to a more buoyant state of contemporary tradition in American fiction:

> Tommy Wilhelm's loss of wife, children, home, job, social status, self-respect, father and fortune constitute, in Bellow's

> scheme of things, the saving circumstances against which the hero must realize his humanity.[31]

Tamkin is a physical grotesque whose twisted body reflects his twisted mind. The reader's attention is constantly focused on his pagoda-like shoulders, peculiarly formed bones, strange brown deceiver's eyes, pigeon-toes and mesmeric mental power:

> Bogus philosopher, self-taught intellectual, false healer and evil Freudian psychologist, Tamkin combines in caricature all the worst perversions of Modernist belief.[32]

Henderson The Rain King the fifth novel of Saul Bellow tells the story of a rich frustrated American. Henderson the protagonist of the novel is the first Gentile presented by the novelist. He is an Anglo-Saxon millionaire of New England Protestant family. He is recipient to a large heritage of wealth, historical responsibility and social service, a massive access to the history of American and Western culture. Henderson imagines what the bystanders speak about him:

> Do you see that great big fellow with the enormous nose and mustache? Well, his great-grandfather was secretary of state, his great-uncles were ambassadors to England and France, and his father was the famous scholar Willard Henderson who wrote that book on the Albigensians, a friend of William James and Henry Adams.[33]

When he thinks about and accounts for the immense proportions of his nose, he recalls that "I was once a good looking fellow...." Besides, his bulky body, huge wealth and wide learning of politics, finance, science and history, Henderson is also a world traveller both as a soldier of World War II and also as a civilian. He has lived in England, France, Italy and Germany. On the whole Henderson becomes the symbol of an affluent Western Culture.

Henderson is representative of "boundless desire" which is the symbol of American way of life. He says that every afternoon he hears an inner voice and when he tries to suppress it, it becomes stronger and it says only one thing, "I want, I want!" He tries to satisfy it with so many comforts but he is not successful:

> I would walk it, I would trot it, I would sing to it or read to it. No use.[34]

Henderson does not know what he wants. He only knows what he has. In such a rich environment of the noble line of the family and property he is shrinking within himself. He is becoming smaller and smaller. He has been a man of high aspirations. Now he has become a victim of frequent humiliation. He says, "Society is what beats me. Alone I can be pretty good and there is the devil to pay."[35] Henderson is so rich and so strong that he cannot submit to the net of society. However, he becomes a broken man. He has been suffering from spiritual malady in the atmosphere of wealth and luxury. He feels that the heart may be empty when the belly is filled. He further realizes that technology extends the promise of an increase of wealth but man starts suffering from the poverty of the soul. Henderson who has been a great fighter in the war and who has won various medals for his heroism is suffering from the poverty of the soul. He complains:

> Ah! it is miserable to be human, you get such queer diseases, just because you are human and for no other reason.[36]

Henderson's rejection of humanity causes him even greater pain.

Henderson's story is the story of the quest of the self. According to Saul Bellow what Henderson is really seeking is a remedy to the anxiety over death. His problem appears to be an existential problem.

Henderson The Rain King is a picaresque tale with several episodes. The first four chapters of the book appear in the form of prologue and they explain the motive of the hero in undertaking the African expedition. Henderson states his case in the opening lines of the novel:

> What made me take this trip to Africa. There is no quick explanation. Things got worse and worse and pretty soon they were too complicated. When I think of my condition at the age of fifty-five when I bought the ticket, all is grief. The facts begin to crowd me and soon I get a pressure in

> the chest. A disorderly rush begins—my parents, my wives, my girls, my children, my farm, my animals, my habits, my money, my music lessons, my drunkenness, my prejudices, my brutality, my teeth, my face, my soul! I have to cry, "No, no, get back, curse you, let me alone!" But how can they let me alone? They belong to me. They are mine. And they pile into me from all sides. It turns into chaos. However, the world which I thought so mighty an oppressor has removed its wrath from me.[37]

The material possessions tie Henderson to the physical world but they seem to stifle his soul. His subjugation to the world of matter makes him wretched in spirit. He cannot feel at home in the company of his two wives. His first wife Frances is an intellectual type of lady "absolutely sold on reason." She is a voracious reader and a great letter-writer. She spends all her time in pouring over books and neglecting the other part of marital life. Henderson says:

> When she got on one of her kicks of philosophy or something I would see very little of her. I'd know she was up in her room smoking Sobraine cigarettes and coughing and making notes working things out.[38]

She is so much preoccupied with books that she cannot afford time and affection for Henderson. Though long-married, her relationship with her husband is still mechanical. Henderson remembers that once while they were visiting France for a year, she preferred to attend "the college de France" where all philosophers were. She neglected her family, she once rushed off to a party in a rude manner and left Henderson behind. She told him that she had got another business of an intellectual nature. Henderson is also a graduate from a university and he feels that the intellectual obsession of his first wife is callous, brutal and terrifying to him. Henderson was attracted towards his second marriage with Lily. She had got seductive charm but aggressive temperament. However, Henderson found that her humanity as well as her personality was more fascinating to him. In choosing Lily who was twenty years junior to him, he surrendered not only to her beauty but also to his quest for a fresh lease of life. With Frances there was no sharing of emotion but with Lily harmony was possible in spite of discords.

Henderson left his wife and children and went to Africa which seemed to be his destination. He admitted in his mind, "All travel is mental."[39] And therefore his journey was not different. Henderson's Africa is the Africa of his mind, it is not geographical and real Africa. Henderson and his native guide travel through dry and barren land and go into deeper heart of Africa. The novelist enables his protagonist to come into contact with two ancient tribes of Africa who stand for the two opposing poles of the American culture of the fifties. The American culture during this period was polarized between two extreme groups, "academics" and "bohemians," "conservative" and "radicals." Bellow calls these hostile forces as "Cleans" and "Dirties." He writes about them in the following manner:

> The history of American literature can be described as a succession of encounters between rival claimants. At the present time there is a sort of struggle going on between the squares and some other shape considered better, or, as I prefer to call it, between, Cleans and Dirties. The cleans want to celebrate the bourgeois virtues...steadiness, restraint, a sense of duty. The Dirties are latter-day Romantics and celebrate impulsiveness, lawless tendencies the wisdom of the heart. The cleans are...conservative and...speak for the Anglo-Saxon majority...the Dirties are...sentimental moralists.

The two African tribes, the Arnewi and the Wariri are cast in the philosophical mould of the Dirties and the Cleans. The Arnewi like the Dirties or the modern American Romantics are governed by the law of the heart. They are irrational, impractical and indifferent to reason. They endorse the simple life of nature, they resent progress and accept primitive life with its tribal setting and elemental laws. The land of the Arnewi is primitive. While entering the village Henderson says:

> I felt like I was entering the past—the real past, no history or junk like that. The prehuman past.[40]

A moment later he again says:

> Hell, it looks like the original place. It must be older than the city of Ur.[41]

Bellow's emphasis on the ancient quality of the land makes the reader believe that symbolically here is the imaginary home of the Dirties. It is obsessed with the idyllic and the past. Like the land its people are also primitive and beautiful. They symbolize the noble savages or the hippies of the fifties. Henderson comments that everybody was good looking and some of them would have satisfied the standard of Michelangelo himself. The Arnewi maintain their primal innocence. They live in an ancient condition. Their houses are made of thatch and mud. Their only occupation is cattle raising. They turn their back on modern civilization. This kind of love refers to the emotional nature of the Arnewi.

When Henderson first turns up in their midst, the village is in the grip of crisis. The land is affected by a drought and the cattle are dying fast for lack of drinking water. There is a pond nearby and the villagers can get water for their cattle from it very easily but they prefer not to take water because the pond is full of frogs. The only solution lies in the eradication of the frogs. The Arnewi cannot do so, they keep sitting idle blaming fate. Henderson tries to convince them that they should face the crisis in a brave manner and do something about the frogs but they cannot do so. The Queen of the tribe, Willatale, and her sister, Mtalba, are also sentimental and have no interest in intellectual life. In this way the Arnewi are prone to superstition, they rely on fate and they cannot think in an independent manner. Thus, all the Arnewi people including their queen represent an emotional and impractical outlook. Bellow uses this tribe to present an allegory about the Dirties.

The Wariri, on the other hand, with their rational and practical outlook represent the Cleans or the Squares of the fifties. When Henderson arrives at their village, he is arrested and put on trial. It shows that the Wariri are guided by a cold rational outlook and are wily and "warlike" in their spirit compared to their meek and humble neighbours. While the

Arnewi represent a vision of innocence, the Wariri present a vision of experience. The first live in an intellectual wasteland and the second in an emotional wasteland. The Arnewi love their cattle "like brothers and sisters" and the Wariri treat and sacrifice their animals without any sympathy. On his arrival Henderson sees many young women preparing their animals for slaughter. On the next day he witnesses the tribals slaying more animals without any compassion. Besides, the Wariri are also vicious in their dealings with one another. They do not hesitate to kill their fellows for personal game. They have got a cut throat attitude which reduces the village to a land of dearth. Henderson spends his first night there with a corpse. The next morning he sees more corpses hanging by the roadside. Compared to their neighbours the Wariri are taken to be more "civilized." They live in large buildings and not in thatched cottages of the Arnewi. The Wariri have also a social system with advisers, soldiers, state officials and ministers. The novelist has drawn the two imaginary African tribes keeping in view the American society and culture. The big boisterous cities with crowded streets stand for Wariri village and New York's Greenwich villages or East villages refer to Arnewi village. In that way the novel is representative of American life in an allegorical manner.

The novelist introduces the episode of king Dahfu who has got a study of modern psychology and medical science, he also appears as a transcendental philosopher. It is through him that Henderson comes to enjoy the vision of reality of death. Henderson is preoccupied by the idea of death all the time. He has been suffering from the fear of the total extinction of his body and soul. King Dahfu takes Henderson to a chamber in the underground where he keeps a lioness named Atti. Henderson is afraid of the sight of the lioness but Dahfu tells him that he should become friendly with Atti. The king is an instructor and he instructs Henderson that a man may become whatever he chooses. Day after day there follows lion lessons with Dahfu. The king tells him that if he acts like a lion, he will take the attributes of a lion, he will achieve a fearless state of mind. Henderson says:

> I would never make a lion, I knew that but I might pick up a small game here and there in the attempt.[42]

Henderson has got a great faith in Dahfu because in his opinion the king faces the world and its reality without fear with the courage of a lion. Dahfu knows "what life and death is." However, Bellow shows that his protagonist is a doubtful student. He cannot share Dahfu's confidence. Even then he may get something out of his contact with the king. The king feels that the lioness is responsible for his strength of spirit. The king wants to capture it. He prepares the net with which he is to make the capture. Dahfu is killed in the lion hunt and Henderson realizes that there is a principle of horror and death in reality. Hitherto, he had not been aware of that. Henderson flies towards home with the cub that is supposed to hold within it the soul of the dead king. On the plane he makes friends with a small boy who is a refugee and an orphan. The boy and the cub are the only companions of Henderson. When the aircraft lands in Newfound Land, Henderson playfully and joyfully takes the boy and the cub and runs leaping and laughing. The episode of the king and the lioness is symbolical. Henderson makes a reconciliation with death. He comes to learn the nature of reality. Henderson has undergone the experiences of death. Now there is a revival of his spirit through this teaching. He returns to Lily and comes to realize the meaning of love again. He develops a fellow feeling for animals. Henderson's return to his family completes his quest for discovering the meaningfulness of human life. He has come to understand human life through much suffering and agony. His reconciliation with reality brings in him a feeling of exaltation. His Lazarus-like rise from death to life is the rejuvenation of his spirit.

In *The Dean's December* Saul Bellow tells us the tale of the two cities, Chicago and Bucharest. The former is a western capitalist state and the latter is an eastern totalitarian state. Albert Corde the protagonist makes a comparative study of the nature of crime and violence in the city of Chicago and the life inside the "iron curtain" in the Communist city of Bucharest in Rumania. Both the cities are equally decadent and degenerating in the opinion of the novelist. However, Bucharest is bleaker than Chicago in grim wintry December. Aged women stand in queues at four in the morning for their limited amount of rations—"a few eggs, a small ration of sausages, three or four spotted pears."[43] Life in eastern Europe is painful due to "forced labour, mental hospitals for dissenters, censorship....Electric shocks, sulfadiazine injection."[44] Under the Communist regime in Bucharest the common life of the people is hard and unhappy. However, people like the Police Colonel "dining in his luxurious villa, eating delicacies and drinking special vintages"[45] live like Texas millionaires. Millions of people pass a closed life from the external world and hanker for freedom in Bucharest. Many of them send their children into the free world of American Universities. Chicago presents a liberal society as opposed to the oppressive society of the communist world. According to the protagonist Chicago is "contempt centre of the U.S.A." dominated by "brutal people." Crimes like "broad daylight rapes and robberies, sexual acts in public places-vandalism running to more than a million dollars a year"[46] are quite commonplace. The Dean further finds that the American ideas of "liberty, equality, justice, democracy, abundance" carry no meaning in America. It is because there is an atmosphere of chaos all round. Thus, Chicago appears as gloomy and decadent as Bucharest because of the forces of evil everywhere.

Albert Corde has given up a good journalistic career in Paris in order to become a college Professor. He is a man of wide learning. He plays the administrative role as Dean of students. He publishes articles on Chicago life in "The Harpers." His motive in writing the articles is not to make publicity but he has cherished "the high intention to prevent the American idea from being pounded into dust altogether."[47] He makes deep research on the Chicago crime and criminals. He interviews the public defender in a murder case where a young housewife is raped and murdered in a cruel manner. In that way he gets involved into the state affairs. As Dean of students he is called upon to examine the murder of a University student named Rickie Lester. The youngman one day went out in the night in search of adventure and "dirty sex" and came back to his apartment with Chicago hoodlums who tied him and pushed him out of the window of his third floor apartment. Rickie Lester died of the injury of a broken skull. The Dean recognised that the death was sudden and unfortunate. The youngman was in the prime of his life and his death indicated the rotten state of life in the city of Chicago. The Dean did not allow the criminals to run away freely, he announced an award for the witnesses who would provide information. As a result of that Lucas Ebry and a prostitute who were both blacks and belonged to the "underclass" were caught on the basis of the information. Albert Corde was ready to meet the challenge of the militant students in the campus. His own nephew Mason who was the son of his widow-sister got angry with the Dean because his friend had been charged with the crime of murder. He made an appeal to his uncle not to wage a war against "the underclass." The trial of the criminals caused great sensation in the city of Chicago because the Dean was determined to get the criminals punished. In the meantime Albert Corde further published a few articles on the sad conditions of prisoners in the country jail. In that way he incurred the displeasure of the high class men even then he was out to expose the darker life of Chicago in which broad daylight rapes and robberies were common. Corde was further shocked by the death of a youngman in the presence of his wife in his own apartment. He offered his sympathy to the mourning wife. All these events of death made him study the violence and crime which had poisoned the so-called civilized life of the city.

Albert Corde also studied the scene of death in the socialist Rumania. He discovered that the authorities of the Communist party interfered with the common human life behind "the iron curtain." Valeria the minister of Health in the Communist regime had been condemned publicly thirty years ago. She had welcomed the Russian soldiers with roses and had been sent to prison as a result of that. Later on, she became a doctor in the hospital. She did not make a compromise with the authority and sent her talented daughter to America to earn recognition as a scientist. The Communist party became inimical towards her and the mother would not meet her daughter without official permission. Albert Corde had married her daughter Minna. Valeria the old woman died at a mature age on the Christmas Day with total consciousness. She had become blind and paralysed but she reacted to the Corde's words "I also love you Valeria." She must have been satisfied to hear such words from Corde and she must have felt the security of the marital life of her daughter. Valeria died in a peaceful manner while Lester became a victim of senseless violence, Valeria overcame the evil thrust upon her by the Communist regime by her loyalty, integrity and her consciousness of death. Valeria's death did not point to the total destruction of spirit for the Dean who stated "Valeria was certainly dead. She had died.... But he couldn't say that she was dead to him."[48]

In the novels of Saul Bellow the protagonists often go through an experience of death and in that way they come to understand the meaning of death:

> To accept death is to accept life—we must endure our going hence even as our coming hither, ripeness is all.[49]

This is the attitude of Keats towards death and the novelist endorses such view of death. Albert Corde compares the two types of death in the city of Chicago and in the city of Bucharest. He observes that in the western world of Chicago death has lost its importance. Through the observation of the hero the novelist analyses death in a physical and metaphysical manner.

The novelist takes up the issue of family disintegration after the death of Valeria. He shows that in Chicago the family life is almost crumbled down but in Bucharest the bond of family relationship among Valeria, Gigi, Minna and other relations had remained intact. The Dean had also been admitted as a member of this big family:

> Here everyone was kind—family and friends, warm hearted people.[50]

Minna was deeply attached to her mother. She mourned her death and became almost heart-broken. The mother-daughter relation is a fine example of filial love in spite of the fact that both of them were living in two different continents. The novelist seems to assert the institution of marriage as a foundation for stable life. He appreciates the virtues of tolerance and understanding among the members of the family. The Dean's relation with his family in the beginning was not very happy. It was feared that the Dean would not make a good husband because he had made love to so many women in his youth but later on he came to learn the lesson of stability and peace in his marital life. He had now become a dependable husband and had got rid of his "erotic collapse." The importance of the Dean in matters of family relations is increased all the more when we come to learn that the protagonists of Bellow are often at war with their families.

In his intellectual and philosophical search the Dean concentrated on the problem of death and he was able to transcend the fear of death in a philosophical manner. He accepted life which appeared to him to be more meaningful than death. The novelist in this way has taken up so many social and spiritual problems such as the problem of love and marriage, the problem of crime and violence, the problem of the preservation of individual rights and the problem of life and death. Prof. Corde who has resigned from the post of the Dean has become Platonic and comes to examine the nature of reality and the shadows of reality. In this way the novelist touches so many aspects of human life in this novel through his men and women.

More Die of Heartbreak tells the story of a world famous Botanist Benn and his disastrous marriage with Matilda Layamon. She is a beautiful and an avaricious lady. Kenneth the narrator is the nephew of Benn, he is self-absorbed and self-appreciating. He cannot look to the other side of things. The novel satirizes a sexual revolution that has taught the people not to take each other seriously in love affairs. The novelist studies a heterosexual relation in which the two opposite sexes start a war against each other. It is also a study of misogynous love stories. When Benn confesses his attraction towards Matilda Layamon, Kenneth is appalled and starts speaking against women. Benn's perception of women is related to the idealization of the beloved but Kenneth is a classical misogynist who considers women to be traditional hags. Kenneth launches the main attack on the educated and powerful Matilda Layamon. He represents her as a woman who will inevitably bring death to her lover. Matilda is presented as a bitch. The philosophy of Kenneth is related to the dissuasion of men from marriage and also from the company of women. He becomes violent in his attempt to dissuade Benn from marrying Matilda Layamon. Bachelorhood and celibacy are prized as morally and spiritually superior to marriage. Benn enters into a secret marriage with Matilda and Kenneth becomes furious. The misogyny of Kenneth remains an ethical problem for male and female readers. Saul Bellow brings into light the gender hostility of Kenneth and presents him as a wraith who cannot cope with the ordinary affairs of human life:

> He has revealed some of the contemporary obstacles to love in enlightening, witty, and even sophisticated ways. However, he has failed to provide a full vision of culpability and rehabilitation. And he has still failed to escape traditional significations of "woman."[51]

Two short paperback novels *A Theft* and *The Bellarosa Connection* were published in 1989. The plot and character of these two short novels differ from the longer works like *The Dean's December* and *More Die of Heartbreak*. The novelist no longer focuses attention on the chaos of society, rather he studies the "messy lives of several neurotic egocentrics."[52] Bellow once again presents the worldly intellectuals more successful in their public rather than in their private lives. Clara Velde and Teddy Regler the two central figures in *A Theft* do not experience the bliss of marriage. The emotional Clara attempted suicide two times because of her unsuccessful love affairs. She got married with "brilliant men" and they had failed Clara emotionally all the time. Her involvement in four loveless marriages made her a broken woman. However, the novelist makes Clara and her lover Ithiel Regler as the subject of his comical novel. The couple in spite of their intellectual powers face grave difficulties in handling the crisis of love and marriage. Clara and Ithiel exhibit a struggle of love affair similar to the one portrayed in *Herzog*. When Saul Bellow was questioned about Clara and her four marriages by the interviewer, he responded by saying:

> Given that forty per cent of marriages these days go on the rocks, you can't blame a lady for trying again.[53]

In their twenty years love affair both of them are involved in extramarital love affairs with great thinkers.

The Bellarosa Connection is full of comic ironies in which the first person narrator refers to himself in the third person and makes judgements and expresses philosophical views about the characters continually. The narrator is a Jewish Mosby in the sense that he divorces himself from all that is personal and emotional involvement with others. The humour and the irony in the novel are similar to those of *Mosby's Memoirs* (1968). For the narrator of *The Bellarosa Connection,* Henry Fonstein, a European Jew who has been saved from the Nazis by Billy Rose is a comic character. The rescue operations were performed by a multi millionaire New York figure who was a song writer in a show. The plot is further developed by the refusal of Billy Rose to meet Fonstein, the man whose life he had saved. Fonstein could not offer thanks to his benefactor. Sorella the wife of Fonstein makes the connection meaningful between her husband and Billy Rose. Sorella presents a picture of the Nazi camp in which "prisoners were sent naked into a swamp and had to croak and hop like frogs. Children were hanged while starved..."[54] The narrator further refers to the plight of the victim:

> I found myself in a hole. Night, a dark plain, a pit, and from the start I was already trying to climb out.... I could see over the edge, but I couldn't crawl out.... I was clawing at the dirt for something I could grip.[55]

The vision of life presented here is sad and gloomy.

Ravelstein (2000) the thirteenth novel of Saul Bellow is full of autobiographical elements. The protagonist is based on the novelist's friend Allan Bloom a philosopher who died of Aids. In this novel the author discloses:

> He has been recently faced with a life threatening illness for which the completion of the novel is a recompense.[56]

The book is an exuberant tale about political ideas and human mortality. Saul Bellow the octogenarian deals with the theme of illness, death and the persistence of the soul which are of great interest for an old man. The whole book seems to be an elegy, however, it turns towards the importance of life in the end. Abe Ravelstein is a young and idiosyncratic Professor of philosophy. He has read a lot but he has written nothing. Chick the narrator of the story is an elderly writer. He suggests Abe Ravelstein to put down his ideas in the form of a book and in that way he plays a part in making him a scholar of world eminence. Originally it is also a financial plan which makes the Professor rich and attracts the attention of thoughtful leaders like Thatcher and Reagan. Ravelstein is dying of AIDS, he makes Chick agree to write a biographical sketch of him. Chick is the picture of Bellow himself who is the superb recorder of the struggle of the mind in America in the modern world. Ravelstein dies and Chick has still to write his biography six years after his death. It testifies to the depth of their friendship that prompted the request. In the late part of the book Chick suffers a breakdown as he has been infected by a fish eaten on a holiday. He has got a hidden fear that his own life will be at an end. Bellow takes the risk of describing the hallucinations of Chick in details. It is just a reflection of the shadow of death hovering over the life of the novelist himself. Bellow writes, "I am a great believer in the power of an unfinished work to keep you alive." The book gets finished and Ravelstein is kept alive, he is summed up in the final image like this:

> He loses himself in sublime music, a music in which ideas are dissolved, reflecting these ideas in the form of feeling. He carries them down into the street with him. There's an early snow on the tall shrubs, the same shrubs filled with a huge flock of parrots—the ones that escaped from cages and now build their long nest sacks in the back alleys....

> Ravelstein looks at me laughing with pleasure and astonishment, gesturing because he can't be heard in all this bird-noise.
>
> You don't easily give up a creature like Ravelstein to death.

Ravelstein is a natural figure in the gallery of Bellow's fiction which has always been strong in the portrayal of heroes who are great thinkers.

Though Saul Bellow has written a great deal about women in his novels yet he is primarily interested in men who possess poetic sensibility and mantic awareness. Most of his protagonists are some sort of poets. They write poems, songs and even psalms in their moments of deep joy or grief. The novelist also uses poetical prose in order to describe their state of mind. These protagonists are also thinkers and philosophers and they make an attempt to discover the true nature of their soul. In worldly matters they are not very successful in enjoying a family life in the company of their wives. These protagonists also represent the contemporary society of America with their various problems. A few women play significant role and seem to possess an independent bent of mind. The novelist seems to express autobiographical sentiments through some of his men and women.

Notes

1. Cronin, Gloria L., "An Introduction to Saul Bellow", *Saul Bellow Society And Journal*, Home Page.
2. *Dangling Man*, 119.
3. *Ibid.,* 153-54.
4. *Ibid.*, 92.
5. *Ibid.*, 154.
6. *Ibid.*, 165.
7. Hicks, Granville. "Distractions of a Fiction Writer,' *The Living Novel : A Symposium* ed. , New York, 1957, 15.
8. Opdahl, 24.
9. *The Adventures of Augie March,* 452.
10. Opdahl, 160.

11. *Dangling Man,* 24.
12. Herzog, 266.
13. *The Adventures of Augie March,* 421.
14. Opdahl, 128.
15. *Ibid.*
16. Chavkin, Allan. "Bellow and English Romanticism", *Studies in the Literary Imagination,* 17, No. 2, Fall, 1984, 7-18.
17. *Humboldt's Gift,* 306.
18. *Herzog,* 1.
19. *Ibid.,* 117.
20. *Ibid.,* 4-5.
21. McConnel, 20.
22. *Seize The Day,* 21.
23. *Ibid.,* 9.
24. Schazler, Brigitte Scheer. 66.
25. *Seize The Day,* 70.
26. Opdahl, 107.
27. *Seize The Day,* 56.
28. *Ibid.,* 104.
29. *Ibid.,* 117.
30. *Ibid.,* 90.
31. Cronin, Gloria L. "The Seduction of Tommy Wilhelm: A Post-Modernist Appraisal of *Seize The Day,*" *Saul Bellow Journal,* 3, No. 1, Fall/Winter, 1983, 18-27.
32. *Ibid.*
33. *Henderson The Rain King,* 7.
34. *Ibid.,* 24.
35. *Henderson The Rain King,* 49.
36. *Ibid.,* 83.
37. *Ibid.,* 3.
38. *Ibid.,* 9.
39. *Ibid.,* 167.
40. *Ibid.,* 46.
41. *Ibid.,* 47.
42. *Henderson The Rain King,* 298.
43. *The Dean's December,* 55.

44. *The Dean's December,* 67.
45. *Ibid.,* 132.
46. *Ibid.,* 162.
47. *Ibid.,* 124.
48. *The Dean's December,* 175.
49 Murry, J. Middleton, *Keats and Shakespeare,* Oxford University Press, 1968, 134.
50. *The Dean's December,* 7.
51. Cronin, Gloria L. *Two Not-so-Farcical Misogynists in More Die of Heartbreak. Saul Bellow Journal* 11.1 (1992).
52. Siegel, Ben. "Love's Labors Lost: Saul Bellow's A Theft". *Saul Bellow Journal* 11-12 (1992).
53. Steinberg, *Publishers Weekly,* 60.
54. *The Bellarosa Connection,* 28.
55. *Ibid.,* 86.
56. Bradbury, Malcolm. *Introduction to Herzog,* Penguin Classics, 2001.

3 Vision of the Woman

The novelist has portrayed a great variety of women who possess contradictory traits and elude any attempt at generalisation. Even the definite attitude of the novelist in this regard remains a matter of controversy. It cannot be ascertained whether some novels exhibit personal attitudes or not. In most of them the marital relations between the protagonists and their wives are not happy and end in divorces. In personal life the novelist has also passed through as many as four divorces and they are likely to affect his vision of the woman to a certain extent. However, a novelist can overcome his personal prejudices and with the help of his imagination present more or less picture of the woman in his work.

Several charges of misogynism have been levelled against Saul Bellow and it is pointed out that he has not done justice to the women characters in his novels. It is also asserted that he has failed to portray convincing women. Leslie Fiedler remarks:

> Indeed, the whole of Bellow's work is singularly lacking a real or vivid female character, where women are introduced, they appear as nympholeptic fantasies, peculiarly unconvincing.[1]

John Clayton also writes in the same vein in relation to *Herzog*:

> The women are creations of Herzog's masochistic imagination, not 'real' at all.[2]

In this context it may be admitted that the fictional technique of Bellow does not allow him to portray women directly as they are perceived through the minds of the male protagonists "who often overshadow them."[3] As the narrators are generally men going through various existential crises, the female characters in comparison, often do not have the same depth of emotional, moral, and intellectual complexity as the heroes or anti-heroes. Bellow does not accept such adverse criticism. In this context it is pertinent to point out that he has tried to convince interviewers of his high regards for his heroine Clara Velde. He informed one reporter:

> Clara Velde is a composite of all the women I have known. I had a love affair with her in the writing. I was all charged up about her. I took great satisfaction in getting close to a uniquely female intelligence. I've often experienced this intelligence, but for some reason, I've never thought of writing about it. Then I reminded myself that, after all, I did know a great deal about ladies.[4]

A very intriguing fact is that Bellow is as sensitive to woman as to man. Though his novels are male-centred, they are also peopled with women of all sorts, "modern 'new' women and traditional old-world women, brilliant women and shallow materialistic ones, aging women who are trying to remain "girls" and young women who try to appear older...." Bellow appears to be advocating freedom for women, their realization of selfhood and tries to explain their behaviour in psychological as well as sociological terms. He is also interested in illuminating certain societal attitudes towards women rather than fully painting their characters. His attitude towards women appears to be self-contradicting and paradoxical. He seems to be a feminist and anti-feminist at the same time. He maintains a balance between feminism and anti-feminism. On the one hand he shows the disintegration of the family caused by ladies like Madeleine and on the other hand he expresses his Jewish faith in holding the unity of the family through women. His picture of women is full-blooded and wholly alive. It is to be examined whether these contradictions are real or apparent, whether Bellow is taking the middle line between the two opposed attitudes. It is also worthwhile to find out whether Bellow's Jewish identity affects his portrayal of women or not. It should be further analysed whether Freudian psycho-analysis in which Saul Bellow's women are studied, restricts the portrayal of his women characters or not.

Iva is the central woman figure in *Dangling Man.* Her personality is overshadowed by her husband Joseph whose consciousness forms the main theme of the novel. The reader learns about Iva from Joseph's angle of vision. She is not heard speaking in her own voice. She is young and energetic and she wants to lead a life in which her freedom might be maintained. She has been working as a librarian and Joseph, who is out of employment, lives on her salary. She proposes that Joseph should devote his time in writing his book on Diderot and should not try to seek new employment. Joseph has resigned from his job in the American Travel Bureau to respond to the Army's call for induction. As it is delayed he has to depend on his wife's salary which makes him think that he is "kept" by her. He feels that Iva's family has been accusing him of living at their daughter's expense. This embarrassing situation creates a state of tension between Iva and Joseph. Besides, Joseph who remains preoccupied with the learning of books cannot like the superficial interests of Iva such as "clothes, appearances, furniture, light entertainment, mystery stories, the attraction of fashion magazines."[5] He makes Iva read books of his choice and Iva does not like it. Iva is also fond of learning and she spends long hours in the midst of books and periodicals at the library. Therefore, she needs books of light reading at home for the sake of entertainment. Her husband cannot understand her point of view. The situation becomes further worse when both of them fall out on the question of the lost book which is not really lost but which has been given to Kitty Daumler towards whom Joseph is attracted. Joseph is disappointed to find that another lover has displaced him in the heart of Kitty. He turns silently to get reconciled with Iva. Joseph reasons with himself that women like Iva cannot resist the temptation of cheap things. They follow "superfluous" path because they have not been taught better. He does not try to understand Iva in terms of the inner feelings of a woman. By and by Joseph comes to discover his own self and also understands the nature of Iva. He realizes that the freedom of Iva might be as dear to her as his own freedom. He further comes to learn that the search for freedom is the common desire of all the people. He concludes that the desire for "pure freedom" is the same among men and women:

> the differences in our personal histories, which hitherto meant so much to us...become of minor importance.[6]

He also admits that his attempt to improve the taste of Iva was a mark of male domination over the female. He comes to gain a new insight in the concept of freedom and shows greater understanding and respect for the personality of Iva:

> It was not evident that Iva did not want to be towed. Those dreams inspired by Burckhardt's great ladies of the Renaissance and the no less profound Augustan women were in my head, not hers. Eventually I learned that Iva could not live in my infatuations.[7]

The novelist seems to express his view through his protagonist that Iva is something more than a docile wife, she has got an independent personality of her own and also a taste of her own. Joseph must accept her ways of life in order to maintain a cordial relation between them. Saul Bellow exalts the position of woman through the personality of Iva and seems to advocate for her freedom from excessive male domination.

A feeling of sympathy for women is also aroused by the introduction of the episode of the Servatius party. The novelist describes the victimization of a girl through the device of hypnotism. He wants to show how inhuman cruelty is sometimes practised on the females by the males. 'The old Joseph' as he called himself, had been idealistic. He had admitted after Hobbes that man might be "nasty, brutish" unruly and animal-like and hence, he stood in need of being tamed. However, Joseph had found a remedy of such cruelty in the form of friendship. He had formed with his friends 'a colony of the spirit' or a group whose members could get rid of the vices of spitefulness, bloodiness and cruelty but he discovered the hollowness of his ideal at a gathering of the colony in Servatius party. He was shocked to discover how his cultured friends indulged in the act of cruelty upon a woman. Minna Servatius had become drunk because of marital troubles.

She was disturbed by her husband's flirtation with Gilda Hillman and therefore she demanded to be hypnotised by Morris Abt who had been her previous lover and whom she had rejected years before. Abt had also been a friend of Joseph. He was seeking revenge on Minna who had been his former sweetheart. When she was under hypnotism, Abt cruelly pinched her hand, claiming she would feel no pain but "the skin where he had twisted it, remained white long afterwards."[8] He made her shiver from the cold and asked her how many drinks she had had. She became "aware of the insult" and suddenly sat up and screamed for her husband. The sight of Minna was pathetic and the white marks on her skin left by Abt's pinching filled Joseph with a sense of rebellion. The novelist does full justice to womenfolk by exposing male cruelty and male exploitation of women.

In *The Adventures of Augie March* the hero is shown involved with a number of women but none of them seems to possess a personality of her own except Thea Fenchel. Other women have been introduced to fulfil the purpose of the Bellow hero Augie who wants to discover the meaning of life through love and sex. Sensuality is an essential part of the hero's amorous ventures and his philandering. The hero's rejection of one woman in favour of another seems ridiculous and also heartless. The novelist suddenly plucks Augie out of familiar Chicago and puts him into the exotic world of Mexico with Thea. The novelist also refers to the fact that Thea had conceived the idea of the hunt from "reading articles by Dan and Julie Mannix, who actually had gone to Taxco some years before with a trained bald eagle and used the bird to catch iguanas."[9] Thea Fenchel appears on the scene and makes a proposal for a journey to Mexico. She attracts the hero while showing the prospect of an exotic life and iguana hunting through the taming of a wild eagle. Both of them run off to Mexico in search of love and adventure. Sophie Geratis a former beloved is left behind and Augie is lured by the idea of wild adventures and also by his sensuality:

> Like a strong brush the excitement went over me and I stood up to it with shut eyes of pleasure, heat snarls at the ears and thrills descending my legs.[10]

The hero makes a total surrender to the sensual love of Thea and comes to regard her as his goddess. For the time being love becomes the sole profession of both of them. The lover cannot make any resistance to the schemes of his beloved in his stage of self-abandon. He commits himself sincerely to satisfy all her desire. He is aware of his servility to Thea and is ironical about his own weakness "because I was threaded to her as if through the skin.... I was never before so taken up with a single human being.[11]

Thea appears to be barbarous and eccentric in the pursuit of wild adventures. Iguana-hunting in the Mexican deserts through the tamed Caligula becomes an overiding passion and obsession with her. The hero wants to take her away from her senseless adventures of wild animals through the passion of love but fails in his venture. Thea is a beautiful and crazy woman. She cannot get rid of her ruthless eccentricity. She has been described as a more ambitious lady than Madeleine Herzog. However, her ambition in the hunting expedition is not fulfilled therefore she moves on to the catching of snakes. Augie is offended and remains tormented inwardly. He says, "But I know that, both in love, we were not quite the same in our purpose."[12] He cannot submit to the wishes of Thea and go for snake-catching, rather he takes shelter in the study of books. His sensuality makes him spend a night with Stella and Thea comes to learn it. Their relation is broken and Augie deeply hurt by it is almost crushed. His love affair with Thea comes to a bitter end all of a sudden.

The novelist refers to another aspect of the life of Thea. She is an excessively rich woman. She keeps her dollars in the refrigerator and Augie goes on spending her money in a lavish manner. In doing so he has to surrender to the whims and caprices of Thea. He cannot escape from her clutches but becomes free with her money. He starts earning money through gambling and the economic corruption remains there in his life for some time. The novelist seems to show the evil effect of the excess of money which is in possession of Thea. She cannot be blamed for that. She is the only source of money and she does not drive the hero into the state of dissipation and degradation.

In this way we come to learn about Thea only through her association with the hero and not directly. The male figure becomes the central to the novel and the females are confined to the periphery.

The novelist attacks the lust for money through the person of Margaret who has been described as the nagging and the exploiting wife of Tommy Wilhelm in the novel *Seize The Day*. The novel portrays a single day in the life of the protagonist who is in his middle forties. His relation with his wife has been broken. Even then she goes on draining money out of him in a merciless manner. She swindles him constantly for a bigger alimony. The hero wants to be released from the bondage of his former wife and he wishes to adore his catholic mistress Olive, "the small pretty dark girl" but he cannot be allowed to enjoy such freedom. He condemns the materialistic society which worships the God of Wealth. He himself faces the problem of money but he has a feeling of repulsion towards money:

> How they love money, thought Wilhelm. They adore money! Holy money! Beautiful money! It was getting so that people were feeble-minded about everything except money. While if you did not have it you were a dummy, a dummy![13]

His annoying wife is responsible for creating in him such an attitude towards money. The crushing problem of money caused by his separate wife has made him physically emaciated. He says, "I'll be struck down by suffocation or apoplexy because of her."[14] He proposes to start a new life through the rejection of the world of money and money-minded people but he is helpless. In this way it is through the reaction of the protagonist that we come to learn about the nature of Margaret who pesters her husband for money even after the failure of marriage.

In *Henderson the Rain King* the novelist introduces Frances and Lily who happen to be the two wives of Henderson. They are fictional prototypes of the two opposing poles of the fifties of America. They represent two extreme phases of the American culture known as "Cleans" and "Dirties." Henderson himself is a hybrid of the two. Frances is dominated by an intellectual quality that forbids the display of emotion. Her excessive practical outlook deprives her of tender feelings which are generally shown by a wife towards her husband. Henderson remembers how she laughed at him brutally when he was returning from the war and told her that he still wanted to be a doctor:

> Frances opened her mouth, usually so sober, not to say dismal and straight, and laughed at me, and as she laughed I saw nothing but her dark open mouth, and not even teeth, which is certainly strange, for she has teeth, white ones.[15]

The violent laugh of Frances exposed her perversity of nature and the darkness of heart. Her intellectual qualities which were symbolic of the culture of the Cleans had made her poor in the natural qualities of love and affection. Unlike Frances, Lily represented the irrationality of the Dirties. She was "totally sold on emotion." Her sentimental nature made her hasty, unsteady and reckless. Her rashness was reflected in the way in which she married her first husband whom she hardly knew before her marriage. She divorced him very soon because she had failed to make an adjustment with him. Her rashness was further demonstrated when on the very first day of their meeting, she expressed her love for Henderson. She married a man named Hazard again without sufficiently knowing about him. She left him suddenly and returned to Henderson. Besides being impetuous Lily was given to many dirty habits. Henderson recounts them in these words:

> I learned she had many negligent and dirty habits. She forgot to wash her underthings until drunk as I was, I ordered her to. This may have been because, she was such a moralist and thinker, for when I said, "wash your things," she began to argue.... The earth itself is like that, corrupt.[16]

Her instant reference to the earth in explaining her personal conduct shows her obsession with the moral philosophy of the Dirties who were given to the Romantic dream of returning to the "earth" shunning modern civilization.

Of several women who pass through the life of Herzog, Daisy, Sono, Madeleine and Ramona deserve particular mention. They are mostly known through the views and the experiences of Herzog. Bellow cannot give his female characters the force and power of his central figures, however, these women are not mere creation of his mind as it is sometimes pointed out by a few critics. They have got a life and blood of their own. Daisy the first wife of Herzog has been described:

> a cooler, more regular, a conventional Jewish woman. Herzog had photographs of her, too, in his foot locker under the bed, but there was no need to examine pictures, he could evoke her face at will—slant green eyes, large ones, kinky, golden but lusterless hair, a clear skin.[17]

She is a country girl and as such she possesses freshness and purity of pastoral atmosphere. "From her bare neck and shoulders he inhaled the fragrance of summer apples."[18] The novelist refers to the virtues of her character and praises her for being very systematic and methodical. Perhaps she appears to be the symbol of the early academic life of Herzog when it was free from the sexual storms and mental tortures. The novelist writes about Daisy:

> She was childishly systematic about things. It sometimes amused Moses to recall that she had a file card, clumsily printed out, to cover every situation. Her awkward form of organization had had a certain charm. When they were married she put his pocket money in an envelope, in a green metal file bought for budgeting. Daily reminders, bills, concert tickets were pinned by thumbtacks to the bulletin board. Calendars were marked well in advance. Stability, symmetry, order, containment were Daisy's strength.[19]

Herzog feels guilty for deserting Daisy with whom his life had been systematic and free. He regrets how he had been a bad husband. He had treated his first wife Daisy in a miserable manner. He himself states:

> By my irregularity and turbulence of spirit I brought out the very worst in Daisy.[20]

His marriage with her was broken because he has a preference for a life of uncertainty and ecstasy in amorous ventures. Daisy is a reflection of Herzog's academic life. She is part of Herzog's personality:

> As long as Moses was married to Daisy, he had led the perfectly ordinary life of an assistant Professor, respected and stable. His first work showed by objective research what Christianity was to Romanticism.[21]

Sono the Japanese girl who has already entered the life of Herzog is the precise antithesis to Daisy. She is warm, loving, subservient and admiring. As a young girl she had gone to live in Paris and she was caught there in the atmosphere of the Second World War. She was down with pneumonia when the American troops entered there. She was still sick when she was repatriated, however, she no longer cared for Japan, her rich father allowed her to study in New York. She told Herzog that she was not sure that she believed in God. If Herzog did so, she would also try to have faith. On the other hand if Herzog was a communist, she was prepared to become the same. She responded to all sorts of the moods of Herzog:

> But often he sat morose, depressed, in the Morris chair. Well, curse such sadness! But she liked even that. She saw me with the eyes of love.... [22]

But Sono took care specially of his sensory needs:

> She loved massages, believed in them. She had often massaged Moses, and he had massaged her.... She had a tender heart.... [23]

Sono's massages are direct appeals to the senses of Herzog. Herzog says, "To tell the truth I never had it so good. But I lacked the strength of character to bear such joy." Sono is symbolic of the sensual nature of Herzog. She fails to content the inner self of Herzog. Happiness cannot be found in the indulgence of the senses. "She did not answer my purpose. Not serious enough."[24]

Madeleine the second wife of Herzog is the most significant figure among the female characters of Saul Bellow. She is also known through the mental reverie of Herzog. He gives us a vivid portrayal of her character. He makes an attempt to be an objective observer of Madeleine but he presents only his subjective view. As he is a hurt ex-husband who has been abandoned by Madeleine for his best friend, he cannot be expected to offer a detached and disinterested view of her contact with him. However, we come to learn a great deal about Madeleine through his observations and personal comments. In his opinion Madeleine happens to be a woman of "considerable intellectual power." She also possesses "the will of a demon." Her will is always triumphant and imposing on Herzog who remains mostly passive. He cannot stand his ground against her:

> Madeleine, too, had great charm, and beauty of person also, and a brilliant mind. Valentine Gersbach, her lover, was a charming man, too, though in a heavier, brutal style.... Herzog himself had no small amount of charm. But his sexual powers had been damaged by Madeleine. And without the ability to attract women, how was he to recover? It was in this respect that he felt most like a convalescent.[25]

Madeleine appears as an arch-deceiver in the novel. She has been called an adulterous and vengeful bitch-wife. Several characters inside the novel refer to her bitch-like manners and behaviour. While still married to Herzog she carries on secret love affairs with his best friend Valentine Gersbach. She does the same to Herzog what he has done to his former wife Daisy. Herzog had also chosen to have an affair with Madeleine during the period of his marriage with Daisy. In love affair she is cold-hearted and manipulative. She does not love Herzog though he loves her deeply:

> Theirs was not a marriage that could last. Madeleine had never loved him. She was telling him that. "It's painful to have to say I never loved you. I never will love you, either," she said. "So there's no point in going on."
>
> Herzog said, "I do love you, Madeleine."[26]

Madeleine is a beautiful, ambitious, impervious young woman who has married an elderly Professor and scholar of forty-four. She is clearly aligned with those characters in *Herzog* who are mostly males and whom Herzog calls "Reality Instructors." These characters want to "punish Herzog with the lessons of the real."[27] They want to educate him in the harsh and tough ways of the world from which he has protected himself. Such shielding is characteristically "feminine." Wilson rightly remarks:

> Herzog seems to experience a measure of the general American male anxiety that to be a poet, writer, intellectual, or "sensitive person" is actually to be a "woman."[28]

Critics have often complained that there are no "real women" in *Herzog* and this points to the failure of the characterization of women. Herzog is an important character "in the female realm" of the novel:

> "The feminine" is embodied most powerfully in *Herzog* not in female characters but in the consciousness of the hero, where it resides as a kind of internal woman or internal mother.[29]

The mental obsession of Herzog, his mental suffering, his pathetic condition in being a cuckolded husband, his delicacy of feeling, his philosophical reflections amounting to lamentation make him an important figure of "the female realm" of the novel and hence *Herzog* becomes a study of female consciousness. From this point of view Herzog is more feminine and Madeleine is more vigorous and masculine.

> The strain of the second divorce was too much for Herzog. He felt he was going to pieces-breaking up—and Dr. Edvig, the Chicago psychiatrist who treated both Herzogs, agreed that perhaps it was best for Moses to leave town.[30]

The divorce has caused deep mental tortures to Herzog and throughout the novel he goes on making a struggle to get rid of this obsession. Madeleine lies at the root of the matter. He is always haunted by her memory and cannot enjoy peace of mind. Madeleine emerges in this way as the central figure in spite of the fact that she has been represented through the mind of Herzog. If she is divorced from the mind of the protagonist, the plot of the novel cannot advance further.

Several characters in the novel admire Madeleine in one way or another. They also speak about her ferocious temper of mind. Some women praise Madeleine highly. Geraldine Portnoy says of her:

> She is so vivacious, intelligent, and such a charmer...it is extremely exciting to talk with her, she gives a sense of a significant encounter—with life—a beautiful, brilliant person with a fate of her own. Her experiences are rich, or pregnant....[31]

The above statement brings into light Madeleine's qualities of head and heart. She is open, frank, intelligent and delightful in her dealings with other people. She possesses human and intellectual qualities. Her talks are pleasant and entertaining and they are capable of attracting the people. Joanna Russ comments that in general, "a woman who competes with men, finally becomes—have we seen this figure before?—a bitch. Again."[32] No doubt, Madeleine has been called a bitch by several persons but they all admire her strength of character as well. The lawyer Sandor Himmelstein tells Herzog that she is

> a strong-minded bitch, terrifically attractive. Loves to make up her mind. Once decided, decided forever. What a will power. It's a type.[33]

Further, he starts making arguments with Herzog:

> She's less of a whore than most. We're all whores in this world, and don't you forget it. I know damn well I'm a whore...I realize. At least the eggheads tell me so. But I bet you a suit of clothes you're a whore, too.[34]

It is stated that as a child Madeleine had been sexually abused and her father had motivated her for being vengeful with men. With the result she had become very aggressive. Her sexual frigidity towards Herzog might be the result of her ill treatment by the people. Herzog prefers to consider it an act of "bitchiness" on her part.

The conflict between Madeleine and Herzog is also caused by their scholarly temperaments. Herzog complains, "She's built a wall of Russian books around herself...in my bed." In his opinion their conjugal privacy has been invaded by the studies of Madeleine. Herzog had not realized how Madeleine's love of books would go to affect their married life. There is an element of antagonism between their marriage and the studies of Madeleine. She is a brilliant Radcliffe graduate and as such she feels that her family life does not provide her ample scope for her intellectual development. She wants to pursue her career further for mental growth but there are so many interruptions in her academic life. Her husband cannot take interest in her scholarly temper of mind. He is much more interested in his personal studies, researches and writings. He wishes that Madeleine should share his academic problems and enlighten him as far as possible. Herzog himself admits that Madeleine herself is going through a stage of crisis and is "rethinking everything." She is a woman in conflict in so far as she is living with a husband whom she does not love. At the beginning of her marriage she had expected that her husband would make some room for her academic career besides his own. But she found that Herzog continued to show no interest in her studies. On the other hand he wished that Madeleine should offer him help in his book on the Romantics. He further wanted that she must forgo her own intellectual pursuits for the sake of the academic achievements of her husband. When this is not done he feels thwarted, cheated and frustrated. Madeleine is totally indifferent to the studies of Herzog and her husband also exhibits the same apathetic attitude. When his friend Shapiro asks him the title of her thesis he tells him that he does not know what her research is about. He answers in a vague manner that it is something related to "Slavonic languages" or "Russian religious history." Yet he expects her to know everything concerning the new book he is writing. He regards Madeleine as a brilliant scholar and has got great faith in her intellectual judgement. As Madeleine can show no interest in his work, his male chauvinism becomes evident. He wanted to discuss difficult points of Rousseau and Hegel with her because he knew that she was competent enough to do so but she always evaded the issue. He also did the same "many times and far into the night" when she was speaking on her research subject, he was feeling drowsy and sleepy and he befooled her by giving an impression that he was listening to her discussion but really he showed no interest. Herzog also felt that Madeleine was more homely in her conversation with Valentine who was also interested in her as a person and as an individual. A feeling of jealousy was created in his mind when he found that Madeleine neglected him for dear friend Valentine.

Madeleine's conversation with Shapiro is known through the remembrance of Herzog. We come to learn about her intellectual interests and we are surprised to hear how vast knowledge of Russian history, the Revolution of 1848, of Bakunin, of Kropotkin and of other related figures of Russia she possesses:

> Madeleine and the dignified visitor were talking about the Russian church, Tikhon Zadonsky, Dostoevski, and Herzen. Shapiro made a great production of learned references, correctly pronouncing all foreign words whether in French, German, Serbian, Italian, Hungarian, Turkish, or Danish, snapping them out and laughing-that hearty, sucking, snarling, undirected laugh, teeth moist, head worked back onto his shoulders.[35]

Shapiro himself was a learned scholar. He knew the literature of every field, he read all the publications, he had accounts with book dealers all over the world. When he found that Madeleine was not only a beauty but was also a scholar preparing for her doctoral examinations in Slavonic languages, he said, "How delightful!" Herzog watched his wife as she revealed the wealth of her mind to Shapiro. She and Shapiro talked to each other excitedly and laughed joyfully during their exchange of ideas and it made Herzog jealous. He resented that Madeleine never laughed with him in that carefree manner. He also felt "they found each other exceedingly stimulating."

In his state of jealousy Herzog wants to exercise exclusive possession of the mind of Madeleine. In his opinion she must reveal her mind and thought only to him and not to Shapiro. Herzog admits to himself that he did not show interest in

Madeleine's subject of research as Shapiro had been doing. Madeleine had got enough of confidence in Shapiro. She was always "bursting with ideas and feelings" in his presence. She knew it full well that her thoughts will be appreciated in a genuine manner. Herzog did not join their company all the time, if he sat there:

> He looked like a clunk, bored, resentful, he proved he didn't respect her intelligence. Now Gersbach always boomed along in conversation. He was so emphatic in style, so impressive in his glances, looked so clever that you forgot to inquire whether he was making sense.[36]

Madeleine looked at the sullen face of Herzog and was deeply hurt to find that Herzog did not enjoy their lively conversation. It appeared that he disdained her work and himself wanted to shine all the time. He never allowed an opportunity to her to shine academically in society. Meanwhile, Shapiro went on complimenting her on her wide knowledge and she felt happy and flattered. She had hoped that her husband would bring a change in his attitude towards her scholarly achievements. He would not ignore the fact that other people in society made a deep appreciation of her knowledge. Herzog regarded Shapiro and Madeleine's intellectual discussions as something trivial. He feared that Madeleine was ambitious enough to oust him from the academic world and take his place in the learned world. He reflected:

> It was quite a funny twist of events, Shapiro. While you and Madeleine were tossing your heads, coquetting, bragging, showing off your clean sharp teeth—the learned badinage—I was trying to take stock of my position. I understood that Madeleine's ambition was to take my place in the learned world. To overcome me. She was reaching her final elevation, as queen of the intellectuals, the castiron bluestocking. And your friend Herzog writhing under this sharp elegant heel.[37]

Herzog was of the opinion that Shapiro was more interested in the physical beauty of Madeleine rather than in her mind. He also hinted that it was mainly her beautiful "behind" that he was really involved in.

Keeping in view the affairs of Madeleine with Shapiro, Herzog did not welcome his suggestions and got infuriated when Shapiro proposed to him that they should move to Chicago for proper studies of Madeleine. Herzog said:

> Fill your big mouth with herring, Shapiro!...and mind your own fucking business.[38]

Herzog cannot take such steps for satisfying the ambition of his wife. As he has got contemptuous attitude towards her studies, Madeleine was bent upon pursuing them more eagerly and more intensely in order to show that She could be successful. Herzog thought that it was cruel competition between them. "Madeleine, by the way, lured me out of the learned world, got in herself, slammed the door, and is still in there, gossiping about me."[39] Prof. Ada Aharoni is critical of the attitude of Herzog towards Madeleine and justifies the stand taken by the lady in this respect. She writes:

> As if there were only one place in the academic world and that she has to throw him out, before she can usurp that place! Her knowledge is so threatening to him that he would much have preferred to keep her unlearned. From his point of view, if she has a thirst for knowledge he is ready to introduce her into his own intellectual pursuits, and does not understand why she does not accept his benevolent offer and discard her career in favor of his.[40]

Madeleine has been called by some critics as something unsympathetic, cold, unstable and neurotic. Leslie Fiedler in *Love And Death In The American Novel* says that Madeleine "seems a nightmare projection bred by baffled malice, rather than a realized woman, and Herzog's passionate involvement with her remains, therefore, unconvincing." It may be stated that Herzog's "passionate involvement" is the central theme of the novel and if it is not convincing, the novel *Herzog* would not be the masterpiece of Saul Bellow and it has been acclaimed to be the greatest creation of the novelist. It is Herzog's preoccupation with the passion for Madeleine which makes her a lifelike and powerful character. Further, Madeleine cannot be charged for being "cold" and "unstable." It is because these are certainly

> the symptoms of the unfulfilled and unsatisfied woman, who feels she is not given the opportunity to "grow," and much of her frustrations stem from the fact that Herzog thwarts her intellectual drives and goals. Furthermore, certain critics, such as John Clayton, seem to overlook the fact that in stressing only the negative aspects of her character, they have probably been influenced by the hurt ex-husband's view.[41]

The studies and intellectual aspirations of Madeleine have suffered a setback on account of antagonistic attitude of Herzog. Edvig the psychiatrist asks him why Madeleine passed through a state of crisis, Herzog admits that it might have been caused by his contempt of her intellectual attainments and Madeleine must have felt that she had been neglected by her husband in this matter. Herzog speaks to Edvig about it:

> Something about the books, maybe. Interference with her studies. If I say the house is dirty, it stinks, she thinks I'm criticizing her mind and forcing her back into housework. Disrespectful of her rights as a person.... [42]

The intellectual pursuit of Madeleine must have been a compensation and a substitute for her lack of emotional fulfilment in the company of Herzog.

In view of Herzog Madeleine happens to be a dominating and cruel woman. He also remembers that Madeleine describes him as a tyrant:

> she says you were a dictator, a regular tyrant, you bullied her.[43]

Their accusations are reciprocal and they have some amount of justification. In this context the comment of Jack Ludwig seems relevant when he says that Bellow must be aware of the fact that Herzog is not much more moral than Madeleine and Gersbach. Madeleine writes to Herzog making a complaint that when she was in the room with him he "seemed to swallow and gulp up all the air and left nothing for her to breathe."[44] Herzog further expresses the opinion of Madeleine about his character:

> I was overbearing, infantile, demanding, sardonic, and a psychosomatic bully.[45]

Madeleine also states that Herzog has affairs with other women. Her charges are well founded as it is evident from Herzog's conversation with aunt Zelda:

> you've been reckless about women.
>
> Since Madeleine threw me out, maybe. Trying to get back my self-respect.[46]

Apparently Herzog seems to be a sufferer because of the attitude of Madeleine towards him. He is an abandoned husband. However, he regrets that he has caused so many troubles to other women in the same manner in which Madeleine has caused him. He regrets that his past attitude towards Daisy his first wife has been somewhat cruel. He again thinks that his behaviour towards Sono his Japanese mistress has also not been just. He is responsible for preventing her from going to Japan and in that way making her disobey her father. When Sono had been suffering, he did not go to see her condition even once. So he also inflicts sufferings on other women and Madeleine alone cannot be blamed for this. In spite of such realization Herzog is very much pained and bewildered by the attitude of Madeleine towards him. He regards himself as the benefactor of Madeleine and says:

> Madeleine's particular benefactor. He had done everything for her—everything![47]

Madeleine does not like such patronizing attitude. Rather she makes fun of the expression of such act of benevolence:

> So now we're going to hear how you saved me. Let's hear it again. What a frightened puppy I was. How I wasn't strong enough to face life. But you gave me love, from your big heart, and rescued me from the priests. Yes, cured me of menstrual cramps by servicing me so good. You saved me. You sacrificed your freedom. I took you away from Daisy and your son, and your Japanese screw. Your important time and money and attention.[48]

The above lines throw light on the character of Madeleine. Unlike Iva, Madeleine is frank and outspoken. Her remarks are sharp and pointed. Her language is witty and ironical. It shows that Madeleine is very much intelligent. She cannot accept the thankfulness and gratefulness expressed by Herzog towards her.

Madeleine has not any close relationship with her parents. She stands in need of enjoying fatherly affection. This is why she gets converted to Catholicism and she discovers in the priest a father-like figure to whom she could talk freely. She also tries to find out in forty-four years old Professor the same fatherly love and affection. She has married this elderly man while she is still in her twenties. She is disappointed by the behaviour of Herzog who always wants to impose his superiority upon her and who also lacks fatherly love towards her.

Madeleine is charged by Herzog with neglecting her domestic duties and remaining busy in her scholarly pursuits. Madeleine retorts that she finds it very difficult to do the work of four servants in the house all alone:

> It needs four servants and you want me to do all the work.[49]

Madeleine is not prepared to accept the secondary position allotted to her in the house by Herzog. A similar situation is also created in *Henderson the Rain King* when Henderson expresses similar attitude towards his wife Lyly. He says:

> I didn't like to see her behave and carry on like the lady of the house, because I, the sole heir of the famous name and estate, am a bum, and she is not a lady—but merely my wife—merely my wife.[50]

Thus, we see that the protagonists of Bellow treat their women as second class citizens. Domestic service is not degrading, it is an integral part of the duty of man or woman but the domineering attitudes of the males associated with such duties are not welcomed by women and they regard it as an act of overhandedness and tyranny.

The novelist shows the harsh and cruel attitude of Herzog towards woman in general. He regards them as vampires which suck the blood. He writes that he "will never understand what women want. What do they want? They eat green salad and drink human blood."[51] In the same tone Tommy Wilhelm, the protagonist in the novel *Seize The Day* cries out that he will never understand "woman are money" which implies that money and woman are on the same level. They are material things, lifeless objects and mere commodities.

Madeleine is capable of living a peaceful domestic life in spite of the fact that she has divorced Herzog. She grows sick of his behaviour within two years of the marriage. She states that for "the first time in her life she knew clearly what she was doing. Until now it was all confusion."[52] That is her attitude towards divorce in the case of Herzog. With her lover in Chicago she enjoys a peaceful life. Her peaceful domestic life brings about a change in Herzog who has gone there to shoot Madeleine and her lover. He finds everything going on well. He realizes that Madeleine does not love him:

> Madeleine refused to be married to him, and people's wishes have to be respected; Slavery is dead.[53]

Madeleine emerges as a "new woman" who makes her own choices:

> who ultimately takes her destiny into her own hands rather than being defeated by a patriarchal society. She embodies in her character and her actions the "free" woman who struggles to achieve her chance of growth and her goal of an independent career, as well as her goal of finding real love. Her true-to-life portrayal, her authenticity, and her vividness make her one of the best feminine portraits of her kind in modern American literature.[54]

Ramona stands in contrast to Madeleine in certain respects. She offers rest and comfort to Herzog for which he has been in search. Ramona invests sex with religious significance and prescribes it as the only therapy for the grief of Herzog. She draws him out of his troubles in a sympathetic manner:

> When he was done...it would be Ramona's turn. You treat me right, I treat you right...Ramona was highly experienced at entertaining gentlemen.[55]

She transforms the miseries of Herzog into "sexual excitements" and turns his grief in a useful direction. Ramona is astonished that any woman should find fault with Moses. Herzog tells her that "he was often a flat failure with Madeleine." On this point Ramona becomes instructive and tells Herzog, "Poor Moses—unless you're having a bad time with a woman you can't believe you're being serious."[56]

While Madeleine is a scholar, Ramona is a sensualist and a "sexual masterpiece":

> Ramona truly was a desirable wife. She was understanding. Educated. Well situated in New York. Money. And sexually, a natural masterpiece. What breasts! Lovely ample shoulders. The belly deep. Legs brief and a little bowed but for that very reason especially attractive.[57]

Ramona owns a flower shop and runs it herself. She possesses a "fragrant" quality in her personality. Herzog praises her in these words, "you're lovely, fragrant, sexual, good to touch—everything."[58] Ramona dresses up in an elaborate way for their sexual encounters:

> She entered a room provocatively, swaggering slightly, one hand touching her thigh, as though she carried a knife in her garter belt. It seemed to be the fashion in Madrid, and it delighted Ramona to come on playfully in the role of a tough Spanish broad.... Her eyes were brown, sensitive and shrewd, erotic and calculating. She knew what she was up to. The warm odor, the downy arms, the fine bust and excellent white teeth and slightly bowed legs—they all worked.[59]

Through the medium of sex Bellow shows that Herzog is deeply bewildered and genuinely disturbed though he may find some peace of mind in a temporary manner. However, in the last analysis sex becomes unsatisfying. The novelist shows the clear debate between the body and the soul, between sensual Ramona on the one hand and the learned Herzog on the other. Prufrock in the poem of T.S. Eliot is also captivated and repelled by "downy arms" and he is fully aware of his plight. Herzog also goes through such experiences in the company of those women who offer him sensual love. However, Ramona is "no mere sensualist but a theoretician, almost a priestess." She wants to give her heart once and for all to a good man and becomes the wife of Herzog. She combines in her person the qualities of a conventional Jewish wife also. She is warm, gentle, loving and having genuine family feelings. She is also an excellent cook. On the other hand she is also representative of a modern woman. She is independent, hard working, intellectual and sexual. Herzog compares her to the Egyptian goddess of fecundity, he calls her a "priestess of Isis." He also admires her independent spirit:

> She struggled, she fought.... In this world, to be a woman who took matters into her own hands![60]

Ramona is a preacher and from time to time she goes on delivering sermons to Herzog. She has also got an ideology of her own. She preaches Herzog that a healthy soul resides in a healthy body. She has absorbed the philosophy of Neo-Freudians who took it for granted that the body is the instrument of the soul. She tells Herzog that the art of love is one of the most sublime achievements of the soul. Again, she teaches him that he may renew his spirit through the flesh. The flesh is a precious vessel in which the spirit rests and therefore the body should not be neglected at the cost of the soul.

Ramona never hesitates to express herself fully before Herzog. She tells him that her feelings for him have got depth and maturity and she has an enormous desire to help him. She further tells him that he is a better man than he knows, he is deep man, beautiful but sad, unable to take what his heart really desires. She says:

> This Herzog, this man of many blessings, for some reason had endured a frigid, middlebrow, castrating female in his bed, given her his name and made her the instrument of creation, and Madeleine had treated him with contempt and cruelty as if to punish him for lowering and cheapening himself, for lying himself into love with her and betraying the promise of his soul.[61]

In her opinion Herzog should try to find the meaning of life not by the disintegration of his family but through the love and union of the family:

> She wanted to add riches to his life and give him what he pursued in the wrong places. This she could do by the art of love, she said, the art of love which was one of the sublime achievements of the spirit.[62]

Ramona thinks that she could restore order and sanity to his life and if she did that it would be logical to marry her. Herzog is delighted by Ramona and he cries out in admiration:

> Bless the girl! What pleasure she gave him. All her ways satisfied him—her French—Russian—Argentine—Jewish ways.[63]

Ramona seems to be successful in her effort to heal up the wounds of Herzog's mind created by the divorce of Madeleine. At the end of the novel Herzog appears to enjoy some peace of mind. Ramona has also introduced a kind of stability in his life and he comes to value the importance of family in the life of man. Herzog prepares a meal for Ramona and picks up flowers for her. He has never done such things before for any other woman related to him. Madeleine has earlier complained that the domestic work for her is a great burden and it demands the labour of as many as four servants but she is discovered doing the same domestic work joyfully in the house of Valentine. In the apartment of Ramona Herzog himself wants to wash the dishes after dinner and speaks out, "there's something about washing the dishes that calms me."[64] Herzog invites Ramona to dinner in his own house where he has cooked a good meal for her, he thinks:

> She would help him with the dishes, and then he'd see her to her car.[65]

Through the relationship of Ramona and Herzog, the novelist wants to express the Jewish ideal of a happy family. He wants to show when the relationship between the couple is harmonious, the domestic work remains no problem. In the words of Prof. Ada Aharoni:

> Ramona has already arrived at the goal of full personhood that Mady was aspiring to. She has already structured her life according to her own vision of authenticity and Herzog admires her for it.[66]

Thus, Ramona offers contrast to the previous women of Herzog in so far as she is voluptuous and well practised in the arts and crafts of love. She has got a philosophy to realize soul through the love of flesh. For her fleshly love is a step towards the cure of mental malady.

In *Mr. Sammler's Planet* the novelist introduces three main women characters—Shula Sammler, Angela Gruner and Margotte Arkin. Shula is the picture of an eccentric woman who is half mad. She has been living along with her father on the generosity of Elya Gruner for the past twenty-three years. He came to Europe after the Second World War and brought them out from the ruins to New York. She is the only daughter of Mr. Sammler. She has got too many oddities in her character. She collects things passionately, she is a scavenger and as such she goes on collecting trash baskets and dustbins:

> The full effect would have been no worse than vulgar if she had not been obviously a nut. She turned up in a miniskirt of billiard-table green, revealing legs sensual in outline but without inner sensuality.[67]

Mr. Sammler is disgusted with her collection of rubbish heap by which she surrounds herself. However, he loves his daughter with Jewish sense of feeling. Shula also adores her father in a crazy manner:

> She thought he (Sammler) was to prosper. He could make beautiful culture. Compose a memoir of the highest distinction.[68]

Mr. Sammler's attitude towards Shula is humanly forgiving and his tender concern for her is quite touching—"if there was a danger of exposure or of hurt, he felt in his own organs."[69] Sammler goes to Israel to rescue Shula from the torture of her husband Eisen. He wants to protect her all the time from anticipated dangers on account of her eccentricities. However, he cannot excuse her insane act of stealing the manuscript of the Indian Scientist. He does not like her attempt at evading the charge of theft made against her. He cannot bear Shula's "theft of intellectual property." His attitude towards the act of theft is repulsive and he considers Shula's act of stealing as something lawless. He cannot exonerate his own daughter from the charge of theft:

> Other people may make new rules as they go along but I will not and you will not put me in that position.[70]

Shula has got double religious association. She is a Jew as well as a Catholic. She was converted to Catholicism during her stay as a refugee in a convent in Poland under Nazi torture. She goes to hear sermons and lectures everywhere. She is the first to ask questions. She is involved in discussing question about faith, ritual and Zionism. She is a Catholic at Easter. Ash Wednesday is observed by her. At night she typed something and sang at her typewriter. She is employed by cousin Gruner who has invented this work for her. Gruner has saved her from her equally crazy husband Eisen in Israel. Shula has returned with Sammler to America after being rescued from Eisen. Shula used to say that her father's life work, his memoir of H.G. Wells made him too tense to live with:

> She had H.G. Wells on the brain, the large formation of a lifetime. H.G. Wells was the most august human being she knew of.[71]

Angela is one of the two daughters of Gruner, the other is not mentioned. She is the symbol of sensual womanhood. She is known for her peverted sex life. Mr. Sammler disapproves of her perversions and her promiscuous sex life. Angela is having an affair with a married man and a father of four children. It results in misunderstanding with her lover. Mr. Sammler does not like Angela's indifference to the death of her father. She has disturbed his peace of mind on his death bed with her contemptible sex ventures in Mexico. Angela sends money to defence funds for black murderers and rapists. Mr. Sammler considers it to be an example of her criminal extravagance. Angela fails in her filial love and filial duties.

Margotte Arkin is the niece of Mr. Sammler on the side of his dead wife Antonina. She is now a widow and hence, Mr. Sammler is very sympathetic to her in her loneliness. He prefers to live with Margotte instead of living with his daughter Shula. He considers Margotte as a good natured woman:

> She was good, she was boundlessly, achingly, hopelessly on the right side, the best side of every human question: for creativity, for the young, for the black, the poor, the oppressed, for victims, for sinners, for the hungry.[72]

However, Margotte has got her defect also:

> High-minded, she bored you, she made cruel inroads into your time, your thought, your patience. She talked junk, she gathered waste and junk in the flat, she bred junk.[73]

She remembers how her husband died in an air crash three years ago. She is fascinated along with Shula with the Indian scientist. Mr. Sammler asks Shula to refrain from involvement with a scientist but he does not resent the involvement of Margotte because he considers it proper after her husband's death in the prime of life. Margotte is also a sufferer in another way. She has undergone persecution under the Nazi regime in Germany because she is a German Jew.

Sammler has made some hard comments on the women student activists:

> Females were naturally more prone to grossness, had more smells, needed more washing, clipping, binding, pruning, grooming, perfuming, and training. These poor kids may have resolved to stink together in defiance of a corrupt tradition built on neurosis and falsehood.[74]

In *Humboldt's Gift* the four women who appear in the life of Charlie Citrine function as reflections and symbols of the mind of the protagonist. Their names are Naomi Lutz, Demmie Vonghel, Denise and Renata. They recount man's progress from his early existence in a state of nature to the development of aesthetic impulses in the present age. The middle stage of man in this progress has been the stage of intellect and reason. Naomi the sweetheart of Charlie represents the mind in its stage of nature. In that stage man saw himself as a part of nature without any distinction wrought by intellect. Charlie recalls to mature Naomi:

> I loved you cell by cell. To me you were a completely non-alien person. Your molecules were my molecules. Your smell was my smell.[75]

And again Charlie says, "when I loved Naomi Lutz, I was safely within life."[76] He also tells her:

> I've often thought...that I lost my character altogether because I couldn't spend my life with you.... If I had been able to hold you in my arms nightly since the age of fifteen I would never have feared the grave.[77]

Certainly, our fear of death comes with our separation from nature and the development of intellect. He loved Naomi in his adolescent days but she remains his beloved for all the time. Naomi belongs to that phase of Charlie's life when he was enjoying poetry. He meets her after thirty years in an unexpected manner. He does not feel worried in expressing his love for her. Demmie the second love of Charlie represents the twilight stage in the development of man in which he is partly in the nature and is partly withdrawn from nature through the development of his intellect. Charlie is passionately in love with Demmie who also takes great care of his professional life. When Humboldt is handcuffed and is taken to hospital, it is Demmie who collects money for his treatment. She does it with the aim of sparing the agony caused to Charlie by the tirades of Humboldt. She dies in an aircrash along with her father during her visit to Latin America. Charlie wonders desolately trying in vain to save the remains of the dead body of his beloved. He cherishes the memory of his "significant dead" in a reverential manner. Charlie values her goodness:

> she was strongly drawn to sick beds, hospitals, terminal cancers, funerals. But her goodness was genuine and deep.[78]

Denise represents man's development of intellect and reason. She is a prisoner of the thriving materialism of the twentieth century. She has been described as a "beautiful, slender, aspiring, martial, boorish"[79] woman and an "up-tight" bitch.

She is associated with Charlie's theatre days when he attained the height of material success. Now divorced, she is bent upon appropriating that fortune from Charlie. Her single minded aspiration is to swindle Charlie and become rich herself. She is excessively worldly and cut off from the inner qualities of emotion, feeling and love. Denise is further given to cruelty and "cannibalism."

Charlie seeks escape from the clutches of Denise and turns to Renata. Renata represents the quality of beauty which is associated with the victory of science. According to the novelist man has confined his idea of beauty to the earth-bound definitions. He can see no further than his earthly existence. In the discovery of beauty man must look beyond nature, he must go beyond the material world. Renata does not like the cultural interest of Charlie. She stands for erotic and sensual life. She deserts Charlie in preference to her millionaire Floozaley. Charlie laments the loss of Renata for a long time. On the whole contact with these women makes Charlie a meditative philosopher who asserts the immortality of soul all through his meditation.

Ada Aharoni does not agree to the classification of women made by Charlie Citrine. She writes:

> In *Humboldt's Gift* we find that the protagonist's "analytical skepticism" towards women is just as bad as Sammler's. Sammler at least was honest, Charlie Citrine is hypocritical and double faced in his dealing with women. On the one hand, he encourages the "passionate hypochondria" of women and presses them to tell him about their "tumors and their swollen legs. I wanted them to tell me about marriage, childbirth, money, sickness and death." And when they duly respond and open their hearts to him, he cynically classifies them "into categories as I sat there drinking coffee." His categories are all denigrating: "They were petty bourgeois, husband-killers, social climbers,...." The women he frequents can in no way compare to the companionship of his male friends such as Humboldt, Shapiro whom he truly respects and esteems.[80]

Charlie's friend George warns him against the bad influence of his wife:

> you're not getting enough air with that woman. You look as if you're suffocating. Your tissues aren't getting oxygen. She'll give you cancer.

Charlie answers him in an ironical manner:

> She may think she's offering me the blessings of an American marriage. Real Americans are supposed to suffer with their wives, and wives with husbands. Like Mr. and Mrs. Abraham Lincoln. It's the classic US grief.[81]

The statement implies that nobody should expect happiness in an American marriage.

Valeria and Minna Corde are two important female characters in *The Dean's December*. Valeria dominates the novel in a way and she appears as a matriarch. Albert Corde is impressed by the "human cooperation among women in a communist society."[82] The novelist describes the feminine network of Valeria:

> There was a love community of women here. The matriarch was Valeria. Ioanna was a member in good standing. This apartment was the centre of an extended feminine hierarchy.[83]

Valeria is a doctor by profession but becomes an administrator more by compulsion than by instinct. She has studied Freud and Ferencze as a psychiatrist. She is liberal minded in her attitude. She has rather allowed her daughter to marry a controversial person like the Dean. Earlier she had expected that Minna would marry a younger man and a scientist but she consented to the will of her daughter. Valeria has studied the long articles of the Dean on Chicago and in that way she has got an estimate of his intellectual ability. Valeria is careful of her self-respect and she is not a compromiser. Her greatness lies in the way in which she faces death in a heroic and peaceful manner. Valeria is a person of exceptional brilliance. She is representative of European culture before the war. She has been devoted to her husband, daughter, her family and her compatriots. The Dean who is an American and an outsider is also drawn towards her.

Valeria's daughter Minna is angry, bitter and impatient on the death of her mother. She is an astronomer of international standing. She is lost in her "astrophysical, mathematical occupations." After the death of her mother, she comes down from the study of space and sublunary matters to her planetary life:

> She is the most independent and high powered woman character we have had till now in Bellow's novels.... Bellow gives us a convincing illustration of what a strong, struggling, working, creating "new" woman is.[84]

She has a brilliant scientific mind. She is fully satisfied with her research work. She is a woman of strong will and intelligence. She is sensitive, thoughtful and kind. She has achieved the goals of an intellectual career and the real love in the company of a husband.

Like other women characters of Saul Bellow Minna is also portrayed through the perception of the male protagonist. Her free voice is not heard. We come to learn about her from the experiences and statements of her husband. We hear her voice only in a very few passages. In spite of Minna's qualifications, Albert Corde seems to mock at her involvement with astrophysics research. The husband often comments that she is more at home "in the stars" than on her planet. There is a conflict in his mind between his social pursuits and the space studies of Minna. He doubts whether she has read his Chicago articles regarding the decline of modern civilization and the growth of crimes in modern life. He wants to drag her in his social problems but is not successful. Minna has got problems of her own, they are related to her research work and the fatal sickness of her mother. He seems to give importance to his own work and prefers a wife who might think and feel exactly like him. When he married Minna, he had known that she was a scientist with a good career and the taste of her own. Albert Corde feels that his wife Minna does not take his articles seriously and does not share his problems. Minna tells him clearly that she would give priority to her own scientific research. Albert Corde regards her research work as something superfluous which has nothing to do with the real life of men:

> She did stars, human matters were her husband's field.[85]

The novelist points to the male attitude towards women in intellectual matters. The statement of Ada Aharoni on this point is very illuminating:

> It is clear that the same male chauvinistic attitude towards the previous women characters is present in the case of Minna too, though her status is much higher than either the librarian Iva or the doctoral student Madeleine. Though she is a world-famous scientist, the protagonist's attitudes towards her is still aggressive and domineering. Corde, before the end of the novel, will learn the same lesson that Joseph did when he realized that "Iva could not live in my infatuation" and that the freedom to pursue one's own personal interests and tastes is a unifying element in human relations.[86]

Minna cannot become the "background" of her husband's "foreground." Albert does not regard her as a human being. She is just like a distant star which communes with the other world. However, he regards Minna as an "innocent" person. He admits that Minna "when she was brought back to earth could be a tigeress." She is just like Denise in *Humboldt's Gift* who is "a great beauty but not altogether human...exquisite and terribly fierce." Minna is a lover of harmonious and peaceful life. She dislikes noise, disorder and publicity. The Chicago articles of her husband which are intended to create great noise go against her nature. Sometimes she pretends that she does not know a subject. Her husband enjoys her company most in that condition:

> She knows him better than he knows her and understands his craving for "macho" superiority, which she nobly grants him, despite the obvious disparity of knowledge and status between them. He is a dean of a college and a journalist, but she is a world-famous scientist.[87]

The death of her mother Valeria causes emotional and physical tensions in her mind. Her relationship with Albert becomes conflicting when she finds that he does not comfort her on this point. She requests him for support at her breakdown but Albert is surprised at her weak nature and on her anxiety over the death of her mother. He is very harsh towards her in making a remark that she has chosen a career among the stars and she has neglected the earth. She cries in despair: "Why do you think you shall tell me this now, Albert? I tell you how horrible my mother's death is, and the way you comfort me is to say everything is monstrous. You make me a speech."[88] Her cry shows that she loves him and expects something from him. She tells him that she finds in him a more strange person than what she had expected. Albert thinks, "you couldn't fathom Minna's conceptions of strange and normal because she was so astronomical. The hours she spent with you, dear heart, were hours among the galaxies." But he admits that at times "she came back from space." At the end of the novel Albert and Minna reach the stage of mutual reconciliation.

More Die of Heartbreak is misogynous in its narrative construction. It is a lament about "failed men and absent mermaids." The characters are comic and the love-lores are misogynous. Kenneth's assessment of Benn's other women is very cruel. He goes on speaking against women in his listening circle:

> While Benn's perception of women is initially a Poe-like idealization of the beloved, and Kenneth's that of the classic misogynist, Dr. Layamon sees women as aged hags.[89]

Kenneth advances his project to deconstruct "women" and romantic love for Benn. He explains to Benn that his spiritual nature attracts educated women very much. His discourses are misogynistic. His intellectual agenda is the first clue to his gender hostilities. He tells the tale of the flight of the bridegrooms from entrapment by marriages. His cruel, arrogant and taunting depiction of women is sad. He talks of erotic teases, whores and rich bitches and in that way he creates an atmosphere of horror. According to Kenneth sex and women are cruel jokes which nature has played on the males. He makes comment on the secret marriage of Benn:

> I didn't take his marriage well, he should have given me advance notice.[90]

The gender hostilities of Kenneth come to notice in his Russian class about "the meaning of love." The curriculum is related to a long historical tradition of misogynous love stories. In such stories the bridegroom-to-be runs out of the window before entrapment into marriage. The speaker tells the listener that love is angelic and it becomes mere carnality in the physical body. Benn makes a counter-thrust to this statement, "Through love you penetrate to the essence of a being."[91] Kenneth disapproves Benn's such views on love which are primitive and pre-industrial:

> Numerous Bellow fictions have lamented the failure of relations among the sexes and shamelessly invoked negative stereotypes of women, but none are quite so bitter as this text.[92]

In this way Kenneth's tirade against women is representative of his misogynous attitude towards women who are misrepresented in his speeches but such statements are exceptional and they cannot represent the general views of the males about women.

In his novel *A Theft* Saul Bellow presents the portrait of Clara Velde who is an affectionate, generous, impulsive, romantic and attractive woman. She comes from Protestant background and has got a highly successful journalistic career. By the age of forty she has established her own "journalistic agency specializing in high fashion for women." She later sold her company to an international publishing group where she has remained a top executive and is considered "a czarina of fashion writing."[93] She now resides with her fourth husband Wilder Velde and their three young daughters. Clara is fortunate enough to do her good job as her husband is unreliable breadwinner. He is large, handsome, lazy and incompetent. He spends time in reading light and sensational books and does not study serious works. Clara has passed through four loveless marriages. Her previous lovers did not satisfy her emotionally but the present one has provided her the needed "masculine bulk." Clara finds Wilder generally compliant and sweet. However, he is mostly boring in the opinion of Clara. Wilder Velde never speaks to the reader, Clara speaks for him. Clara confides in Laura, a Chinese-American dress designer who has no function in the novel other than to listen to Clara. Clara cannot understand her previous lover's philosophical observations and expressions. She is fully aware of her limitations. She says:

> Do not ask me for specifics. I can't give them. They're always flitting by me.[94]

She does not even appear, as Joyce Carol Oates rightly observes: "intelligent enough for her worldly position, nor even for her author's continued investment in her."[95]

Clara went on making matters worse by not thinking much about her marriages. She spent her energies in youth for acquiring "love and happiness" but she got little. At present she lays claim to being a devoted mother. She does not forget her lover Teddy Regler who has become an obsession with her. Clara is painfully aware of the emotional price which she has paid for this love. She is convinced that she has provided him with the emotional support he needed to continue functioning as an important public treasurer. Bellow who always emphasizes the importance of true love to an individual seems to point to that direction. Clara states that her love has given true meaning to Teddy's life than have his significant public achievements.

Clara's previous marriages in the novel are barely mentioned. Each appears to have been more exciting than her present one. There is reference to Spontini, "Mad Mike" who was the third husband of Clara. He was an oil tycoon who accidentally blew himself to pieces with one of his own bombs. There is description of Teddy whose latest wife has just left him with all the house furnishings. Clara consoles him by saying that he should not marry a woman who does not value him. She cannot expect the same fate from him. Clara had pressured

Teddy to buy her a green emerald engagement ring. Later on the ring is lost. She is greatly distressed by the loss, Teddy is not. Clara guesses who has taken the ring. This is the story of the true "thief" in the novel. In Bellow's novels external factors are always at work. Money often causes disputes between the husband and the wife or among the members of the family. Land or property or even a ring may also cause dissension in the family. The ring is found out by Clara and she never returns the money to the insurance company. A more serious theft in the novel is Clara's misreading of Gina's true character. She suspects that the ring has been stolen by her and thereby she rocks the young visitor Gina of her dignity and pride:

> But then perhaps the major thief is Teddy Regler. He has robbed or at least deprived both Clara and himself of a life of shared love and happiness.[96]

At first Clara feels hostile towards Gina but quickly dismisses all resentful thoughts. She owes Gina for getting her ring back and for what she had done for her troubled daughter Lucy. In the episode of the ring the novelist's intention is to reveal Clara's "tender heart" under her tough executive exterior.

The narrator records no ironical reaction to Clara's involvement in four marriages. All of her husbands make odd companions for a sophisticated lady. The main theme of the novel seems to be a struggle between Clara Velde and her lover of twenty years Ithiel (Teddy) Regler. They become the subject of Bellow's comedy. In spite of their intellectual powers they face great difficulties in handling their crisis of love and marriage. Their struggle is just like the struggle of Herzog which in the opinion of Bellow is "portrayal of the American intellectual trying to come to grips with life." The result is a novel which blends the comic and the serious. The novelist describes the mind of Clara with its shape and size. Clara is intelligent with "short blond hair, fashionably cut, growing upon a head unusually big...she needed that head, a mind like hers demanded space."[97] Bellow adds in "an inert character, a head of such size might have seemed a deformity" but in the case of Clara it was not true. To the contrary Clara released "so much personal force" that her large head appeared to be handsome. As the novelist has referred she stood in need of having that type of head which was full of space. In spite of her intelligence Clara attempted suicide two times because of her failed love affairs. Both Clara and Ithiel were involved in extramarital love affairs and that caused a break up in their marriage. The narrator describes Ithiel as having deep feeling for Clara and Clara is excessively a romantic in her attitude towards Ithiel. The emerald ring which for Clara is the symbol of their relationship is also a mark of their depth of feeling for each other. Their relation moves towards a spiritual level of meaning:

> She held the ring to her face, felt actually as if she were inhaling the green essence...still, this emerald also was an ice. In it Ithiel's pledge was frozen. Or else it represented the permanent form of the passion she had had for this man...it was as real as the green of the ocean, as the mountains in whose innards such gems are mined.[98]

When Clara was still single and hopeful of marrying Ithiel, she told him, "I love you with my soul" but her devotion did not deter him from having other "lady friends." When he chastises her for interfering with his life, her plea "Do not go now, I'm in a bad way"[99] does not prevent him from swinging the door shut after him. When he finds out her attempt for suicide, he rushed to the hospital but after a very brief stay, he departs abruptly. In this way Ithiel appears to be hypocritical in his love towards Clara. The romanticism of Clara becomes helpless and in the end she comes to study her authentic self and she draws inspiration from it. Now she is able to face life in a fresh manner. Her inner self provides her strength of character which might enable her to face the problems caused by love affairs. The narrator further describes the communication between Clara and Gina and also between Clara and Lucy. There is a sense of love and sympathy and a feeling of humanitarian outlook. The novel shows Bellow's ability to laugh at character's foibles and at the human condition.

Thus, Bellow paints all types of women who are attractive, fascinating, inspiring, boring, lovers of carnal pleasures, lovers of scholarly life, some narrow-minded, some broad-minded and so on. Some of them are selfish and self-indulgent, a few of them are also odd and grotesque. They stand in contrast to male protagonist's need for idealistic love. A few of them are regarded as obstacles to spiritual growth. Some women are devouring and unreasonable and before them their men appear poor and helpless. These are usually ex-wives such as Herzog's second wife Madeleine.

Notes

1. Fiedler, Leslie. *Love and Death in the American Novel*, New York: Stein & Day, 1967, 363.
2. Clayton, 211.
3. Aharoni, Ada. 99-112.
4. Chambers, Andrea. "At 73, Nobel Laureate Saul Bellow Decides He Wants to Be a Paperback Writer." *People Magazine*, 27 March 1989, 65-66, 69.
5. Dangling Man, 65.
6. *Ibid.*, 102.
7. *Ibid.*, 65.
8. *Ibid.*, 52.
9. *Ibid.*, 334.
10. *Ibid.*, 357.
11. *Ibid.*, 369.
12. *Ibid.*, 407.
13. *Seize The Day*, 33.
14. *Ibid.*, 44.
15. *Henderson the Rain King*, 14.
16. *Ibid.*, 16.
17. *Herzog*, 126.
18. *Ibid.*
19. *Ibid.*
20. *Ibid.*
21. *Ibid.*, 5-6.
22. *Ibid.*, 170.

23. *Herzog*, 167.
24. *Ibid*., 103.
25. *Ibid*., 5.
26. *Ibid*., 9.
27. *Ibid*., 125.
28. Wilson, Jonathan. *Herzog : The Limits of Ideas* published by Twayne publishers, Boston, 29.
29. *Ibid*., 30.
30. *Herzog*, 7.
31. *Ibid*., 99-100.
32. Russ, Joanna. *What can a Heroine Do? Images of Women in Fiction*, ed. Susan Koppeleman Cornillon.
33. *Herzog*, 82.
34. *Ibid*., 85-86.
35. *Ibid*., 70-71.
36. *Ibid*., 72.
37. *Ibid*., 76.
38. *Ibid*., 74.
39. *Ibid*., 77.
40. Aharoni, Ada. 99-112.
41. *Ibid*., 99-112.
42. *Herzog*, 58.
43. *Ibid*., 39.
44. *Ibid*., 191.
45. *Ibid*.
46. *Ibid*., 38.
47. *Ibid*., 124.
48. *Ibid*.
49. *Ibid*., 123.
50. *Henderson the Rain King*, 6.
51. *Herzog*, 41-42.
52. *Ibid*., 100.
53. *Herzog*, 7.
54. Aharoni, Ada. 99-112.
55. *Herzog*, 157.
56. *Ibid*.

57. *Herzog*, 67.
58. *Ibid.*, 152.
59. *Ibid.*, 16.
60. *Ibid.*, 337.
61. *Ibid.*, 184.
62. *Ibid.*
63. *Ibid.*, 200.
64. *Ibid.*, 194.
65. *Ibid.*, 340.
66. Aharoni, Ada. 99-112.
67. *Mr. Sammler's Planet,* 22.
68. *Ibid.*, 93.
69. *Ibid.*, 165.
70. *Mr. Sammler's Planet,* 154.
71. *Ibid.*, 27.
72. *Ibid.*, 18.
73. *Ibid.*, 20-21.
74. *Ibid.*, 36.
75. *Humboldt's Gift*, 302.
76. *Ibid.*, 76.
77. *Ibid.*, 213.
78. *Ibid.*, 164.
79. *Ibid.*, 202.
80. Aharoni, Ada. 99-112.
81. *Humboldt's Gift,* 43.
82. *The Dean's December,* 75.
83. *Ibid.*, 72.
84. Aharoni, Ada. 99-112.
85. *The Dean's December*, 256.
86. Aharoni, Ada. 99-112.
87. *Ibid.*
88. *The Dean's December,* 259.
89. Cronin, Gloria L. *Two Not-so-Farcical Misogynists in More Die of Heart break.*
90. *More Die of Heartbreak,* 50.

91. *More Die of Heartbreak,* 225.
92. Cronin, Gloria L. *Two Not-so-Farcical Misogynists in More Die of Heartbreak.*
93. *A Theft,* 2.
94. *Ibid.*, 89.
95. *Ibid.*, 3.
96. Siegel, Ben. *Love's Labors Lost: Saul Bellow's A Theft.*
97. *A Theft,* 1.
98. *Ibid.*, 43.
99. *Ibid.*, 33.

Technique of Portrayal

4

Bellow's art of portraying characters cannot be reduced to a set rule or a rigid pattern. It is also not conventional or post-modern in its technique. It is independent and indeterminate. It may change from one fiction to another. However, some sort of technique might be discovered in his fiction-writing. Bellow writes, rewrites and revises a novel several times:

> Parts of *Herzog* for example, were written twenty times, sometimes with minor changes, sometimes with major ones. Mastering the right tone of voice, establishing the appropriate distance—these were the essence of revision.[1]

Such attempt might imply the art of selection and precision followed by the novelist but it is something more than that. Bellow freely speaks about the question of revision in a number of interviews. He says:

> The main reason for rewriting is not to achieve a smooth surface, but to discover the inner truth of your characters.[2]

It is obvious that Bellow is a novelist of character rather than of plot or surface. From letters, interviews and articles it is known that Bellow usually begins his novel with one or two characters. His novels are dominated by characters mostly. According to Aristotle plot comes first and it is the soul of tragedy. In Bellow's novels there are also plots and situations but it seems that his characters cannot remain confined to the net of plot and they assert their identities and individualities in an independent way. The characters undergo various stages of transformations. In some of them like Humboldt, the degree is less, in others like Henderson the changes are greater. His protagonists make a quest for the nature of the self and in that way they become the central figures. Their personalities overshadow the persons of female characters. They seem to carry greater weight on account of their metaphysical leanings and spiritual inclinations. There is one thing more and that is the question of maintaining a respectable distance from the characters. Bellow's art forbids him to identify himself with anyone of his characters. The autobiographical elements may be there in the novel but nobody can say that the author is moving behind his character. He does not impose his personal idea on a particular character. He allows him to develop in a free manner. His method is objective and detached, though some kind of subjectivity and references from his personal life may not be ruled out. His characters cover a wider range and some of them move from one continent to another. The scenes mostly take place in New York and Chicago, there is enough of local colour and topical references but the protagonists are also allowed to make a survey of Africa and Europe. Thus, the technique of Bellow admits a larger canvas for the display of his characters.

Bellow has drawn a variety of characters. They may be as different from each other as Augie and Mr. Sammler. They all bear the impact of the personality of the novelist:

> All of the central characters are transformed into Bellow surrogates yet in saying this one is saying that none of them is Bellow himself.[3]

Bellow comments in this regard:

> I'm as distant as I can possibly be, and if I'm not distant enough, I throw the thing away and start over again.[4]

In this statement Bellow possibly refers to those characters who are sometimes quite close to him. He alludes to the problem of distance in *Herzog* and says:

> I thought in Herzog I was having a certain amount of fun at my expense, or if not at my own expense, I was making fun of my own type.[5]

Bellow's obsession with character is seen everywhere in his novels. Character is the point of germination and pinnacle of achievement for him. Bellow says:

> It seems to me that I've been dealing with a new sort of person and that's been the excitement of the books.[6]

It is often alleged that the novels of Saul Bellow have odd patterns and loose associations. In this context it is stated that Bellow himself describes the form of his novel when he says about *Herzog*:

> He was earnest, he had a certain large, immature sincerity but he might never succeed in becoming systematic.[7]

Tony Tanner also remarks about *Herzog* that the novel is "as mismanaged and patternless as its hero's life."[8] Saul Bellow told an interviewer about the structure of his novels:

> My ambition is to start with an outline but my feelings are generally too chaotic and formless. I get full of excitement which prevents foresight and planning.
>
> ... I regret it when I get into trouble: a book two-thirds done and I do not know how it is going to come out.[9]

All such statements point to chaotic and formless structures of his novels but really it is not so. Bellow never speaks last word on a particular point. There is nothing "fixed" and static regarding his conception of art. We may refer to a particular interview regarding this matter:

> Do you outline your novels before writing?
>
> I wish I were able to.
>
> To what extent do you worry about the structure of your novels?
>
> They give me insomnia, but I seem helpless to do anything about it.[10]

The answers are not flat and conclusive, they are puzzling and they point to dynamic character of the artist. They refer to a state of possibility and not to a state of finality. A similar answer has been given in another interview and that shows the real character of art and the artist. The artist cannot be static and rigid in his work of art. The interview follows:

> *SS*. Do you have a prior idea about the shape of your novel depending upon the nature of the subject matter? Or, your novel slowly acquires a form as you write it down?

> *SB*. No, yes and no. I know somehow in my head how it is going to go. And my novel does acquire a form as I am writing it down. I discover all kinds of things as I am writing it down.[11]

The answer "No, yes and no" is quibbling but it is highly artistic. No definite and mathematical answer may be given about art which imitates human nature. Bellow's art is expansive rather than selective, it is inclusive rather than exclusive. There is nowhere centrifugal expansion and inclusiveness. Bellow has also been criticized for excessive character of self-discipline in his creation. He is spontaneous and forceful in his writing but he is also meticulous in his use of words. He calls himself a "very dogged...very persistent fellow." He must "thrash and sift and winnow until I have a clear notion of what I am doing."[12] An interviewer puts the question before him:

> You had attacked novels that lacked concreteness and particularity and turned more or less into abstractions. I'd like to know how you reconcile...?

Bellow answers him in these words:

> Now it may be that the critics of *Mr. Sammler's Planet* are right. I have no way of knowing whether the book succeeds or not, but in my own defense I think it is possible to say that people do not read attentively and are not very willing to undertake hard work. It is hard work, a book like that. Each word is very carefully weighed and connected, closely connected, to the man.[13]

It shows that Bellow is a conscious artist in spite of his natural flow of writing.

Bellow's technique of portrayal may be studied in his representative novels. We may examine it particularly in *Herzog*. There has been a good deal of controversy regarding the pattern and structure of *Herzog*. We have already referred how Tony Tanner had suggested in 1965 that the novel *Herzog* was as mismanaged and patternless as the life of its hero. It may be stated that the life of Herzog might be mismanaged but it is not patternless. The structure and plot of Herzog point to dialectical pattern of Herzog's behaviour and thought. Herzog is caught between his desire for order and his natural tendency for creating chaos. The novel looks "patternless" because the structure is complex. Malcolm Bradbury remarks:

> Of all Bellow's novels, *Herzog* has the most complicated and labyrinthine structure. The text is a flow, moving backwards and forwards in time, shifting through odd patterns and loose associations, allowing the prose to slip by sudden connection, turn of memory, frenzied mental jumps. The book is multi-layered as no other Bellow novel is, mirroring the mixture of contemplation and frenzy which is the stuff of Herzog's own mind.[14]

The pattern is not smooth because the ways of the novel are zigzag and the journeys undertaken in it are sometimes purposeless. Herzog wanders between the two great American cities New York and Chicago. He also makes a futile trip to Martha's vineyard and makes a struggle there with his double burdens: the first is his mental obsession with his adulterous and vengeful bitch-wife Madeleine and the second is his bearing of the intellectual weight of the ideas which are contemporary, historical and philosophical. Herzog is a creature of ideas and language, he has also a quarrel with philosophy. He goes on writing letters to the newspapers, to people in public life, to friends and relations and also to the dead. Letters are further addressed to Eisenhower and Schopenhauer, Nietzsche and Hegel. The narrator sometimes talks in third person and sometimes in first person. All these factors make the novel complex in structure.

The novelist introduces a flashback technique in the writing of *Herzog*. Herzog is all alone and is thinking about the past incidents regarding his marriage and divorce with Madeleine. He enters into a long series of reminiscences on the break up of his marriage. Throughout the novel the activities of Herzog are interspersed with memories and some of the memories return Herzog to his early childhood. The flashbacks and reminiscences constitute the major part of the novel. We may discern from them the nature of the plot and the structure of the novel. The novel has a series of dialectical movement. It is a movement from order to chaos, that is from thesis to antithesis. The clash between the two brings about the synthesis which does not come to a stop in the dialectical process. It again becomes thesis for a new dialectical movement. Three women who play an important role in the life of Herzog may also be seen in the dialectical process. Herzog's first wife Daisy is the symbol of order and his second wife Madeleine is just the opposite. Daisy offered him symmetry and order but life with her was dull and uninspiring. Contact with Madeleine brought about a storm and instability in his life. For the time being a synthesis was discovered in his girlfriend Ramona but it was not final. The novel develops the pattern of a pyramid in the amorous longings of Herzog with his women. The structure is organic and interconnected. Herzog becomes the victim of Madeleine just as Daisy has been the victim of Herzog. Though Ramona promises to restore order and sanity in the life of Herzog yet she does not appear to be successful. Herzog does not make a plan to marry Ramona. She is present in the life of Herzog at the end of the novel but he appears to be a little uncomfortable. Ramona becomes the "thesis" for Herzog's next dialectical movement but the reader does not witness it in the novel.

Saul Bellow also adopts symbolic technique in the writing of his novels. Herzog inhabits most frequently three environments in the novel, New York, Chicago and Berkshires. They function in similar manner to Herzog's three main women. During a conversation on dinner Herzog points quite unconsciously to Ramona different elements of his personality that come into play in New York and Chicago. His personality becomes a divided self in these places. In New York "the man inside" appears to be on the rise while in Chicago Herzog is very much "the man in the street." The symbolic alternatives of New York and Chicago appear to be between stagnation and motion; inactivity and activity, contemplation and action. The novel has got the structure of a tale of two cities in the life of Herzog. However, the tale of two cities also incorporates a house in the country and Herzog's life in Berkshires seems to resolve his internal conflicts. It is just the same as Ramona seems to resolve the conflict of Daisy and Madeleine in the life of Herzog by making a place herself in his life. The house in

Berkshire is a symbolic extension of Herzog's state of mind. From the outside Herzog appears to be successful but very soon the things start going wrong. Madeleine begins to exhibit signs of paranoia or mental disorder. She thinks that Herzog has hired a private detective to follow her and very soon after the birth of their daughter, Junie, she commences her seven years affairs with Gersbach. She brings domestic chaos in the life of Herzog. In Herzog's memories of his life in Berkshires we discover the consciousness of New York and the activity of Chicago. Herzog comes to enjoy some peace of mind only in his second return to this place and not in his first dwelling in the house. His theoretical "synthesis" in Berkshires remains incomplete:

> Herzog still has a long way to go but at least he has arrived in a position, which we might usefully call creative stasis, from which he can prepare to begin again.[15]

Thus, the dialectical structure of Herzog is an important feature of the novel.

The structure of the individual characters in *Herzog* also corresponds to the structure of the novel as a whole. Individual characters who appear to be divided personalities throughout the novel emerge united at the end of the novel. They transcend themselves in certain respects and seem to suggest the view that human being is "more than his characteristics." This idea is applicable not only to Herzog but also to Madeleine and Gersbach. Herzog expresses unfavourable views about these two characters. He describes Madeleine as "proud but not well-wiped," "beautiful but distorted by rage," "a mixed mind of pure diamond and woolworth glass" and "as sweet as cheap candy, and just as reminiscent of poison as chemical sweet acids."[16] There is no room for sympathy and warmth in Herzog's description of Madeleine. The cold-hearted aspects of her personality are also shown in the novel in the way in which she conducts her affairs with Gersbach. Gersbach is also treated in a rough manner in the description of his character. He has flaming red hair and one good leg both of which are conventional signals in the 19th century novels and they point to his diabolic character. Gersbach is hypocritical. He acts as a friend and sympathetic listener of Herzog. He poses to be a go-between Madeleine and Herzog while he is actively engaged as the lover of Madeleine. Herzog describes him as "psychopath" and discovers in him a resemblance to the violent instinct of Hitler. One might feel that such extreme view of Herzog has been inspired by his anger, pain and jealousy. Herzog further describes him as a "Charlatan...with hot phony eyes" or a "loud, flamboyant, ass-clutching brute."[17] The view of Herzog changes when he sees that Gersbach is bathing his daughter in a tender manner. By the end of the novel Herzog enjoys some peace and balance of mind and admits that Madeleine in spite of all her bitchery is a "good mother" and Gersbach is not so bad as he appeared to be. In the final assessment of character of Madeleine and Gersbach it is felt that both of them escape definition and cannot be confined to particular word or remark. Medeleine might "read three or four murder mysteries a week"[18] but she is not a murderous figure. Herzog decides in the end that Madeleine and Gersbach are finally "unknowable" like him:

> They resist his definitions even as he resists theirs, and thus evading categorization they are able to embody not only the "truth" that Herzog comes to—that individuals are more than the sum of their characteristics—but also his more general assertion that "utter clarity of explanation...is false."[19]

We are inclined to accept that Herzog's final judgement of Madeleine and Gersbach is accurate. He makes such statement about them when he has recovered his mental balance. Even Herzog is not free from blame in this matter. Herzog is also found guilty of cheating, betrayal and hypocrisy. He has actually cheated his wives. He comes to realize that the sphere of their sins is the same sphere as his own. He tells Ramona:

> I sometimes see all three of us as a comedy team with me playing straight man.[20]

Some critics are of the opinion that Madeleine and Gersbach are symbolic extensions of Herzog's own personality. It is true that part of Bellow's method of characterization is to flank his protagonist with characters who symbolically extend his personality. However, it seems difficult to understand how Gersbach and Madeleine represent the personality of Herzog. Some traits of their personality may be found in him. The moral sentimentalism in the person of Herzog carries some of the traits of Madeleine and Gersbach. But even in this matter there is nothing like close affinity. Madeleine is sick and tired of the way in which Herzog idealizes his childhood and criticizes his life with her:

> Okay—let's hear your sad old story. Tell me about your poor mother. And your father. And your boarder, the drunkard. And the old synagogue, and the bootlegging, and your Aunt Zipporah...oh, what balls ![21]

Somehow or other the terms which define the characters of Madeleine and Gersbach do not seem to be applicable to Herzog.

Another pattern might also be discovered in the symbolic presentation of character in *Herzog* and it might be called Cartesian. Throughout the novel Herzog is astonished over the fact that in spite of passing through the period of crisis he keeps on a good health. The strength of his constitution works as he says, "obstinately against his hypochondria." Madeleine also calls him "psychosomatic bully." Herzog's healthy body seems to signify that his mental equilibrium is not as disturbed as his antagonists like to make out. There is nothing particularly much abnormal about his state of mind as it is sometimes exaggerated. As a matter of fact Herzog is surrounded by characters who are much crazier than he is. We need only to think of Sandor Himmelstein's plate smashing or Madeleine's controllable shopping sprees.

An emotional alignment of secondary characters may be discovered in the body and mind of Herzog:

> Dr. Emmerich, who gives Herzog a physical, is professional, and as far as he can be, given that there is nothing wrong with Herzog, is sympathetic. Dr. Edvig, Herzog's analyst, is, by contrast, untrustworthy and manipulative. Herzog's 'good brother,' Will, helps to get him patched up after his

> car accident, while brother Shura, who is a shadowy figure in the novel, is seen to be engaged only abstractly with money and power. Ramona, as we have seen, is very concerned about Herzog's body, while Medeleine, with whom Herzog has fraught and infrequent sex, directs her energies into elaborate strategies of deceit. Asphalter, "Herzog's good academic friend," gives Herzog booze and a bed for the night, while Shapiro has only intellectual battles to offer. What thus appears to be symbolically extended in the secondary characters is Herzog's mind/ body split.[22]

His body remains healthy, it is his mind that battles with the internal and external factors. Emmerich, Will, Ramona and Asphalter are characters who support Herzog in all matters. Edvig, Shura, Madeleine and Shapiro are not sympathetic to him, their attitude is antagonistic. Some critics have suggested that Bellow is more successful in portraying secondary characters but he does not give force and power to his female characters as much as he gives to his central figures.

An important narrative technique adopted by Bellow is to make a character witness his own psychic drama. This technique has been perfected in *Herzog*. Here the narrator is the witness of the activity of his own consciousness. Bradbury calls *Herzog* "an unreliable witness" but it is not just. Herzog is truthful in his thought and meditation. He may be inconclusive but not false. Porter Abbott points out:

> Herzog himself is reading Herzog. He reflects upon himself as he would upon a character. Thus, as confined as the book is to the interior Herzog, the mind we hear is continually engaged in trying to gain knowledge of itself by reading the acts it has a part in directing.[23]

Opdahl makes similar observation:

> He makes an object of himself, seeing himself as others see him. But he then makes still another removal from himself: "satisfied with his own severity, positively enjoying the hardness and factual rigor of his judgment, he lays on his sofa."[24]

Bellow follows the device of "silent self-examination" made by his other protagonists also. In *Dangling Man* Joseph writes his diary and examines various aspects of his freedom and true self. He undergoes the process of introspection. In the act of self-observation he comes to the stage of the dissection of his own character in an objective manner. He moves from 'I' to 'He' in gaining self-knowledge, he is keenly intent on knowing "what is happening to him." Other Bellovian characters like Mr. Sammler are also engaged in intellectual preoccupations. Mr. Sammler observes, "intellectual man had become an explaining creature." This statement applies to him most. Throughout the novel he is engrossed in the act of introspection. He is lost in solitary musing which makes him the lonely speaker in his state of monologues. Such is the case with Leventhal who examines the visible and the hidden sides of his inner self. He is burdened by his problem of guilt and self-torture. Under the pressure of Allbee he begins to admit his responsibility in the suffering of his accuser in one way or another. As soon as he recognises his involvement into the matter, he becomes conscientious. He cannot ignore wretchedness of Allbee, he is drawn towards him by his fellow-feelings and his sense of responsibility.

Bellow conceives character as a nexus of impulses and passions. He allows his characters to invent themselves and to forge themselves ahead in the quest of transcendental reality. The character in him is not an object to be seen from outside. It is the character who views himself, churns his impulses and impressions and not the reader or the novelist. The reader comes to learn the inner working of the mind of the character. The author vanishes from the world of his characters. In that way he gains a distance from his creations. The effect of the fiction is not damaged by his being too autobiographical. Bellow feels:

> The opposites must be free to range themselves against each other, and they must be passionately expressed on both sides.[25]

Bellow uses a new technique of using letters composed in mind. They are not put down on the paper and they are never sent to the persons addressed. *Herzog* is full of such letters. These letters reveal the mind and the thoughts of Herzog. They throw light on the character of the protagonist and also on those characters who are related to him. The letters further permit the novelist "to write about the private life of a passive character."[26] They carry private thought into the public realm and give rise to thoughts and memories which are more subjective and more frank. The letters are related to the internal and private experiences of the central figure. The novelist had already introduced this epistolary form in *Henderson the Rain King*. Henderson wrote letters to Lily in which he expressed his inner thoughts. In the letter to Lily, he acknowledges:

> This experience in Africa has been tremendous. It has been tough, it has been perilous, it has been something! But I've matured twenty years in twenty days.[27]

Bellow says that he wrote the last fifty pages of Henderson including the letter at a feverish and exultant pitch.

In the novels *The Adventures of Augie March* and *Henderson the Rain King* Saul Bellow follows conventional form of the picaresque novel. The picaresque mode of narrative admits of the introduction of the innumerable episodes and adventures in the life of the hero. The earlier Bellow-Hero lived a tortured life, constantly divided against himself. *The Adventures of Augie March* transcends the limit and allows the hero to make an exploration of the self through long journeys. Augie March is a true picaresque hero in his quest for survival through struggle. He fulfils Frederick R. Karl's norms of the picaresque—"For the picaro, all situations call for struggle, he can hardly relax."[28] In his pursuit after freedom Augie March chooses a flight for an adventurous life. It is difficult for him to lead a commonplace life. He opts for life which is teeming with adventures. He passes his life on the road in the company of strangers and comes to realize that the life of criminals is hateful to him. His acquaintance with strangers on the way enlarges his understanding of life. He returns to Chicago through a tortuous route after many setbacks. He also spends a night in the jail and gains experiences of such life. The hero of Bellow also searches the meaning of life through love and sex. Henderson is also directed by his inner voice "I want" to undertake adventurous journey, his life in America as well as his adventures in Africa makes the most romantic tale of the present age. The protagonist suffers a loss of spirit due to the loss of material possessions. He is disillusioned with the moneyed civilization. His quest is spiritual and metaphysical. He makes a travel to the wilderness of Africa and he comes into contact with several types of people and civilizations. Out of them he comes to learn something about the problem of death. He makes an existential approach to it and accepts death as an inevitable fact of life. In this way the technique of picaresque novel lends the two novels a beauty and a charm which make them delightful. Their series of adventures become misadventures. However, the protagonists come off these adventures with a spirit of affirmation and a longing for higher things.

Saul Bellow follows the technique of double structure in most of his novels. Two kinds of structure and two kinds of modes are generally found in them. They are traditional and subjective structures, the historical and the confessional modes. There is action in the outer world of the hero and there is tension and inner searchings in the mind of the protagonist. To take the example of Joseph in *Dangling Man* One finds that the hero remains shut in his room thinking about the question of human freedom. He wants to protect the self. At the same time the hero also goes out into the outer world and picks quarrel with the people. The double structure has also been followed in *The Victim*. It develops the form of the double plots. On the one hand Leventhal is involved in his conflict with Kirby Allbee, on the other hand, he wants to serve the family of his brother Max. As a typical Jew he is essentially a family man and his attachment to Mary is much deeper. He depends on Mary's good sense and objectivity for getting the right direction. Apparently he feels guilty for his separation from his younger brother Max due to the break up of the family. Asa whose name symbolically means 'healer' is called by Elena to stand by her in the absence of Max. Thus, the double plots have been introduced in the novel. In *Augie March* the double structure expresses itself in converging and diverging lines of action. Augie runs away from one Machiavellian and embraces the other in his quest for an independent self. His devotion towards his family is a Jewish trait. On the other hand he becomes a picaresque hero in his search for the mystery of life. In *Henderson the Rain King* the fifty-five years old protagonist runs away to Africa in order to find a remedy for his suffering. He comes into contact with the two families Arnewi and Wariri which form the sub-plot of the novel. *Herzog* is also an example of such double structure. On the one hand his life has been described as "mismanaged and patternless" and on the other hand it is full of such actions as his going to the court, his going to Chicago to revenge himself on Madeleine and his meeting with Ramona. Such adventure implies some sort of order. In *Mr. Sammler's Planet* on the one hand there are local stories of crime and violence and on the other hand there is an enquiry into the biological future of man and the possibility of a colony on the moon. *Humboldt's Gift* is again built on a similar structure. As Clayton rightly remarks:

> On the One hand is the experience of distraction, on the other is Charlie's experience of an inner light, in the one world the poet is fool, in the other he is at moments in touch with sacred reality.[29]

Bellow makes an abundant use of irony in the portrayal of his characters. Andrew H. Wright defines an ironist thus:

> He may, as an observer of the human scene, be moved to compassion, disgust, laughter, disdain, sympathy, or horror—the whole range of reaction is evidently his: what distinguishes him uniquely is a rare and artistically fruitful combination of complexity, distance, implication.[30]

Bellow uses irony for "complexity, distance, implication." He presents a comical view of certain characters. Apparently they seem to be serious but they become comic in their vision of life. The irony is born out of the difference between appearance and reality. That which appears to be real is not real. Herzog is a comic portrait of the weakness of an educated man. He is a person of good instincts and noble feelings but he falls into the crisis of marriage. He wants to seek health from his "education" and philosophy but his education becomes little more than a joke. "The learned Herzog is merely foolish."[31] His marriage with Madeleine makes him a ludicrous character. She simply cuckolds him and abandons him for his friend. Herzog cannot get rid of his mental obsession for Madeleine. The "romantic hero" becomes a goose. Herzog had betrayed his first wife for Madeleine and Madeleine betrays him for his friend Gersbach. The irony is powerful and expressive.

Bellow's vision of the world presented by his characters is also ironical. His protagonists seek transcendental reality on the one hand and on the other they are deeply rooted in the world. The attitude is very much paradoxical. Again, his heroes go out to discover the mystery of life. They want to defend their true self but at the same time they maintain their connection with society. They look up for glory of life but they also refer to the absurdity of life. Most of the heroes of Bellow want to come to terms with reality but they find that they are outwitted by reality and they have to reconcile themselves to the fact of ordinariness and death. Joseph laughs at a particular hero of Hemingway but at the end of the novel he gives his option for the same type of life. Similarly Leventhal considers himself to be a victim but he comes to discover that he is also a victimizer. He dislikes violence in human society but he finds that he is himself more aggressive and violent than Allbee, though he is under the impression that Allbee is persecuting him. Mr. Sammler dislikes violence and perversity and later on, he begins to admire both. The black pickpocket is disliked by him but later on, he allows concession for him and he becomes part of his own soul. Further, Herzog does not like the imposition of his will on others but he is doing the same when he wants Madeleine to act according to his desires. In *Humboldt's Gift* there is also ample irony. In the words of Judie Newman:

> Charlie's attempts to buck out of history, to flee the transcendent, are also treated ironically. He argues that he

has to abandon his children in order to do them any real good. He must first seek a transcendent truth. The tables are turned by Renata, however, whose quest for what Charlie always calls "the riddle of your birth" parodies Charlie's own ethereal quest.[32]

Henderson the Rain King is also full of thematic ironies. Henderson has fled his continent in order to find "the wisdom of life." In his quest of reality he is conscious of the fact that he heard a voice that always repeated, "I want, I want." He feels that the voice should have told him "she wants, he wants, they want." In that way he becomes just the opposite of what he had started. He is no longer egoistical, he becomes universal. That is the irony of the situation. Bellow cuts a serious thing by his penetrating irony. The true self of the character is revealed through the ironies. Some of the heroes undergo dramatic changes in their ways of life. The novelist conveys a sense of truth through the use of ironies. The irony in Bellow is aligned with parody, satire and comedy. As Stephen L. Tanner writes:

> Bellow often parodies or satirizes the quest for enlightenment (Henderson is notable instance), but it is parody or satire intended to generate balance, realism and humility rather than to belittle and destroy.[33]

Bellow draws inspiration from psychology in his technique of character-portrayal. There are frequent references to Freud in his fictional works. Some of his characters also use the technical language of Freudian psychology. Like many writers and intellectuals of modern age, Bellow was genuinely involved with the process of psychoanalysis. However, in his play *The Last Analysis* he presents a parody of analytical method. His central characters have resisted one or another aspect of Freud's ideas since *The Adventures of Augie March* (1953). The basis of Bellow's argument with Freud is expressed in his two interviews which he gave in the late seventies. Bellow makes it quite clear that his main objection is related to the unconscious which is taken by Freud to be a form of determinism. In his first interview he asks the question:

> What is the unconscious after all? The unconscious is anything human beings don't know.... Is it possible that what we don't know has a metaphysical character and not a Freudian, natural character? I think that the unconscious is a concept that begs the question and simply returns us to our ignorance with an arrogant attitude of confidence, and this is why I'm against it.[34]

Again, Bellow cannot endorse Freudian view of character determinism. According to Freud character is essentially fixed by the age of six. Further, he holds the view that character does not change deliberately, that childhood experiences are of great importance and their effects are unconscious. The root of the problem for Bellow is the nature of the Freudian unconscious:

> Bellow has learned from Freud but essentially opposes him. To say that Bellow knows Freud very well is no exaggeration. There was a period when Freud was his nightly bedtime reading, and Bellow's frequent references to Freud in his fictive works, his notebooks, and his essays reveal an easy intimacy not only with major works but also with minor ones.[35]

Bellow does not give us a positive unconscious. He may not deny the existence of the unconscious but he seems to deny the Freudian character of the unconscious. Bellow wants to express feelings without symbols but Freud cannot do without symbols. For Freud dreams are the language of determinism. Bellow suspects the symbolic interpretation of dreams. In his opinion such explanation is an abrogation of free will. It is a way of exercising the tyranny of the unconscious over the conscious. It is with these reservations that we may study the characters of Bellow who sport with Freudian psychology.

Herzog likes to play with the vocabulary of psychoanalysis in summarizing his own character. He is "narcissistic" and "masochistic" and he accepts Dr. Edvig's characterization of him as a "reactive depressive." At the end of the novel Herzog describes his release from Madeleine in psychoanalytic terms that he has derived from Freud's paper *Mourning and Melancholia*. He speaks about himself in these words:

> But this intensity, doesn't it mean anything? Is it an idiot joy that makes this animal, the most peculiar animal of all, exclaim something? And he thinks this reaction a sign, a proof, of eternity? And he has it in his breast? But I have no arguments to make about it. "Thou movest me." "But what do you want, Herzog?" "But that's just it—not a solitary thing. I am pretty well satisfied to be, to be just as it is willed, and for as long as I may remain in occupancy."[36]

Sometimes Herzog seems to act according to Freud's conception of a civilized person. In the opinion of Freud a person has to pay a heavy price for his civilized behaviour. Herzog draws inspiration from Freud's text *Civilization And its Discontents*. In this book the civilized world has been described as a place where human beings are painfully and inevitably caught between their values on the one hand and their desires on the other. In Herzog the ideas of Freud are recapitulated as the rewards of civilization, these are law, order, civilized behaviour and they are won at the cost of great individual frustration. At times it seems that the psychology of Herzog has sought inspiration from Freud's assertion that civilized man has sacrificed much that would make him happy. In this sacrifice the sexual and aggressive impulses have also been controlled. Happiness implies a sense of security and protection.

After the break of his marriage Herzog experiences misery and frustration. They appear to be the product of his repression of the desire for revenge. The idea is typically Freudian. Herzog has to satisfy himself with the thought of violence. He cherishes the idea of mental murder and it may become a case of psychoanalysis. In his fantasy he imagines what he would like to do to Gersbach and Madeleine who have betrayed him in matters of love and marriage:

> What if he had knocked her down, clutched her hair, dragged her screaming and fighting around the room, flogged her until her buttocks bled. What if he had ! He should have torn her clothes, ripped off her necklace, brought his fists down on her head.[37]

Freud and Bellow differ from each other in their conclusions which they draw from their observations of the human condition. For Freud "unhappiness" is born out of neurotic misery. For Bellow as he shows in the case of Herzog the "unhappiness" is brought on by repression. Its character is not permanent, it is sporadic. Herzog is able to detach himself from his insides into his own misery, he also transcends the state of misery. He does not deal with his problems by confronting Madeleine and Gersbach and talking matters with them. He comes out of his anger and unhappy state by a feeling of goodness and grace.

Herzog's mental conception of the murder of Gersbach and Madeleine becomes a point of debate between Bellow and Freud. According to Freudian concept psychology is interested not in the person who committed the crime or the murder, it is interested only in discovering who desired it and who welcomed it. From Freudian point of view Herzog is to blame in this matter because he is instigated by a desire to do it. However, from Bellow's point of view or from the Jewish outlook the person is not guilty if he has thought of murder, he is guilty when he has actually committed the murder. In this way there might be a point of conflict in the assessment of the character of Herzog. There is a crucial difference between Herzog's desire to commit the murder and his decision not to do it.

In *Mr Sammler's Planet* the introduction of the black pickpocket who displays his penis to Mr. Sammler becomes the subject of Freudian studies. The Negro pickpocket asserts Freud's thesis on the primacy of sexual power. The phallic symbol is psychological and it throws light on the miserable condition of American society. It refers to general "madness" of western culture. It is a symbol of pickpocket's "assertion of power" which is connected with evil forces.

In *Henderson the Rain King* there are frequent references to Freudian symbols of dream. The novel has a close resemblance to the state of dream:

> Freud interprets the dream and the jest as a discharge of powerful psychic energies, a glimpse into the abyss of the self.[38]

Dream and joke are an upsurge from the unconscious. Both of them are a means of exploring the dark realm of the mind. Bellow used Joseph's actual dreams in *Dangling Man* to reveal the truth denied by Joseph's conscious mind. Leventhal's dream in *The Victim* is related to Wilhelm's daylight experience in *Seize The Day*. The same technique has been anticipated in *Henderson the Rain King*. The whole of the continent is converted into a waking dream. Bellow's technique of the symbol of dream makes the novel serious and comical at the same time. Africa which cures Henderson is dream-like. America is also the same which drives Henderson to Africa. Henderson's world is dream-like because he too denies the body and the facts of death. He says:

> If this body, if this flesh of mind were only a dream, then there might be some hope of awakening.[39]

In his dedication to this hope he is indeed a dreamer who sacrifices his real life for an artificial one. He tells us, "I have never been able to convince myself the dead are utterly dead." Every morning wearing a red hunting cap, he retires to demonstrate the immortality of man. He devotes the whole of his life to his dream of transcending life. It points to the artificiality of his existence. The dream symbol in this way is running through the novel but there cannot be elaborate interpretation of dream as it is done in Freudian psychology. However, references to dream have got psychological touches.

Bellow's language which is the means of portraying a character differs from one novel to another. It is reportorial in *Dangling Man,* naturalistic in *The Victim,* symbolic in *Henderson the Rain King,* lyrical and philosophical in *Herzog* and joyous and entertaining in *The Adventures of Augie March*. Besides, it is rich in imagery and symbolism. It is infinitely varied and expressive. Again, it is witty, humorous, ironical, satirical and allegorical according to the temper of a character. Sometimes it becomes learned and erudite as it is required by a character.

Bellow's characters are mostly 'round' according to the division of E.M. Forster. They are allowed natural development and are not sacrificed for the sake of achieving an idea. This is how Bellow answered an interviewer who questioned him about an affirmation of an idea through a character:

> *Interviewer*: Mr. Sammler's Planet seems to me to suggest an affirmation of the terms of life all men hold sacred in their hearts....
>
> *Bellow*: Well, let we try to answer that question. I am interested neither in affirming nor denying anything. A "character" has his own logic. He goes his way, one goes with him, he has some perceptions, one perceives them with him. You do him justice, you don't grind your own axe. I have no axe to grind, one way or the other. This man seemed to me to be the sort of man to whom this would be happening : he happens to have religious feelings.
>
> I did not choose such a person for the purpose of expressing my own religious convictions. I was simply following the thread of his being. I found a clue and I was winding it up, going inwards. It brought me to religion. If it had brought me elsewhere, I'd have written something else. One doesn't arbitrarily invent these things in order to put anything across. That's what I am trying to say to you.[40]

Notes

1. Fuchs, Daniel, *Saul Bellow: Vision And Revision*, Affiliated East-West Press Pvt. Ltd., New Delhi, 1992, 53.
2. Enck, John J., Interview with Saul Bellow, *Studies in Contemporary Literature* 6, 157.
3. Fuchs, Daniel. 53.
4. *Ibid.*
5. Robinson, Robert. Interview, "Saul Bellow at Sixty," *The Listener* 98, 218.
6. Robinson, 219.
7. *Herzog,* 4.
8. Tanner, Tony. *Saul Bellow,* 89.
9. Steers, Nina. Interview with Saul Bellow, Successor to Faulkner ? *Show* 4, 37.
10. Enck, John. "Saul Bellow: An Interview." *Wisconsin Studies in Contemporary Literature,* 6, 1965, 156-60.

11. Singh, Sukhbir. "A Talk with Saul Bellow." *Saul Bellow: The Man And His Work,* ed. by M.A. Quayum & Sukhbir Singh, B.R. Publishing Corporation, Delhi, 2000, 83.
12. Cushman, 141.
13. Kulshrestha, Chirantan. "A conversation with Saul Bellow" *Saul Bellow: The Man And His Work,* ed. by M.A. Quayum & Sukhbir Singh, B.R. Publishing Corporation, Delhi, 2000, pp. 51-52.
14. Bradbury, Malcolm. *Introduction to Herzog.*
15. Wilson, Jonathan. *Herzog The Limits of Ideas,* 42.
16. *Herzog*, 299.
17. *Ibid.,* 102.
18. *Ibid.*, 73.
19. Wilson, Jonathan. *Herzog The Limits of Ideas,* 46.
20. *Herzog*, 190.
21. *Ibid.,* 124.
22. Wilson, Jonathan. *Herzog The Limits of Ideas,* 90.
23. Abbot, H. Porter. 264-83.
24. Opdahl, 156.
25. Bellow, Saul. "Where Do We Go From Here : The Future of Fiction," *Michigan Quarterly Review*, Winter, 1962, 27-33.
26. Opdahl, 155.
27. *Henderson the Rain King,* 282.
28. Karl, Frederick R. *Yale Review* 57/2, Winter, 1968, 200.
29. Clayton, 265.
30. Wright, Andrew H. : *Jane Austen's Novels: A Study in Structure,* Relicom Books, 1972, 28.
31. An Interview with Saul Bellow by Matthew C. Roudane.
32. Newman, Judie. 39-52.
33. Tanner, 288.
34. Boyers, Robert. "Literature and Culture : An Interview with Saul Bellow," *Salmagundi* 30 (1975): 23.
35. Fuchs, Daniel. "Bellow and Freud," *Saul Bellow in the 1980's A Collection of Critical Essays,* ed. by Gloria L. Cronin & L.H. Goldman, Affiliated East-West Press, Pvt. Ltd., New Delhi, 1992, 27.
36. *Herzog*, 340.
37. *Ibid.,* 10.
38. Sypher, Wylie. *Comedy,* 198.
39. *Henderson the Rain King,* 265.
40. Kulshrestha, Chirantan. "A Conversation with Saul Bellow," *Saul Bellow: The Man And His Work,* ed. by M.A. Quayum & Sukhbir Singh, B.R. Publishing Corporation, Delhi, 2000, 54.

Conclusion

5

The major lines of enquiry pursued in this study may point to Saul Bellow's vision of the woman in general. The woman in his novels is neither degraded nor exalted. She stands midway according to her merit and worth. Bellow's vision of woman is truthful and realistic. He has drawn all types of women such as scholarly women, ordinary women, devoted women, apathetic women, eccentric women, normal women, traditional old women, modern "new" women, materialistic and lustful women, spiritually elevated women, sexually indulgent and sexually frigid women, sensitive and insensitive women, kind and cruel women and so on. Some of the women are the mental creations of the protagonists and some women have got real life and blood of their own. Bellow's artistic technique imposes some kind of reservation on the portrayal of women characters. With the result we perceive those women through the minds of the male protagonists and not directly. They often overshadow them. Again, the narrators are generally men who are engaged in existential and transcendental problems. The female characters do not share the same depth of emotional and intellectual problems. Hence, they are eclipsed by the central male figures. Further, we get an impression that Bellow is more interested in illustrating societal attitude towards women rather than painting their character himself.

There is a common charge that Bellow is a misogynist, that he is masochistic and chauvinistic in his attitude towards women. The feminist critics point out that his novels "usually construct an implied male reader or narratee" and this narrative construction nearly always eclipses the female voice and ultimately creates within itself "the narrative conditions of a misogynous collusion of men against women."[1] Such charges are not relevant and just. Bellow's personal life may be full of a number of divorces and his novels may show frequent cases of divorces, marital disputes, cases of adultery and treachery in love but the attitude of the novelist is not governed by these factors. His outlook is universal and not parochial. His canvas of woman-portrait is larger and it admits of all kinds of women with a spirit of toleration. His character-portrayal of women is not "fixed" and static, it is dynamic and all pervasive. Therefore, the charge that Bellow has failed to deal adequately with "femininity" is not true. Bellow shares the complexity of this supposed failures with so many male writers of the time. He is not to blame exclusively in this matter.

According to feminist critics the fictional world of Saul Bellow is populated primarily by men. It is full of social interactions of males only. The males happen to occupy all the major roles while women function on the sidelines. "They are nearly always described in terms of their utility to the male enterprise and are most frequently treated with suspicion and hostility." "It is also stated that "the damaged and/or contaminated male protagonist enacts a celibate, monastic retreat from the sexually chaotic and destructive influence of 'woman' to retake the masculine domain of thought and values." Again, it is referred that "woman" becomes the object of combined gaze of both male author and male reader. "It is a gaze split between a passive female who is looked at and an active male who looks."

The above mentioned charges are much exaggerated. Bellow gave importance to male voice in his novels because of certain factors. He entered the decade of 1940's as a young writer. He came to realize that it was a Hemingwayesque model "of masculinity with its hard boiled, understated existential stoicism that dominated the values and the masculine voice in American literary culture. His decision to write against the grain of this modernist formula has enabled him to stage an entirely different male voice and set of values."[2] Bellow explained the purpose of his own writing in these words:

> ...I am going against the stream. That's not an attitude. Attitudes are foolishness. It's just that there's no use doing anything else is there? I blame myself for not having gone hard enough against it, and if I live I shall go harder.

It is the dominant mood of later modernist despair that Bellow wanted to go hard against with his masculine voice. Bellow has strongly opposed the cultural ideas of western civilization such as "apocalyptic romanticism, a destructive Faustian individualism, cultural elitism, existentialism, alienation ethics, absurdism, nihilism" and aloofness. With this end in view he introduced male protagonists whose masculine voices would be powerful enough to fight against these things. Hence, his novels are dominated by male voice which is conditional and situational and it cannot be taken to be a neglect of the female voice.

Bellow's portrait of woman is objective and free from personal prejudices. The novelist has drawn a faithful picture of woman through his observations and also through his power of imagination. His vision of woman is not fragmentary, it is all-sided and it takes into consideration all the aspects and accomplishments of a woman. More than anything else Bellow seems to be attracted by the intellectual qualities and academic pursuits of a woman. These things are very much found in the personality of Madeleine. Though she pursues a parallel love affair while being married to Herzog yet she does not become an object of hatred by the novelist. It is because the novelist points to similar loose sexual affairs of Herzog also and gives an impression that the male is in no way better than the female. Thus, Saul Bellow does not start traditional war on a woman simply because she is given to sexual appetite and indulges in several love affairs. As referred earlier in the chapter *Vision of the Woman* Bellow has expressed his attitude towards woman with particular reference to Clara Velde in the novel *A Theft*. He regards Clara Velde as "a composite of all the women" and says that he has fallen in love with his heroine in the novel. He also appreciates unique female intelligence in her person. Thus, Bellow is equally sensitive to man and woman. Besides, Bellow advocates freedom for a woman and he also wishes that a woman must realize her selfhood.

As pointed earlier Bellow maintains a balance between feminism and anti-feminism. As a novelist of Jewish tradition he holds fast to the ideal of the integration of the family. It is possible only when the woman follows the ideal of high morality and she remains devoted to her family in a sincere manner. Again, Bellow does not approve of the role of such woman who becomes an agent in bringing about the disintegration of a family. Again, it may also be noted that the Jewish identity of Saul Bellow prevents his portrayal of woman to a great extent. As a Jewish writer he cannot allow full freedom to a woman, his attitude is a bit traditional and the woman in him must occupy a subordinate place to man in the family. As the character of society is patriarchal the woman is unable to revolt against it. With the result the woman in Saul Bellow must occupy a subordinate place but such place is honourable under the Jewish tradition. In *Dangling Man* Iva is something more than a doll, she has got an independent character and taste of her own. Joseph is allowed to accept her ways of life in order to maintain a cordial relation in the family.

The novelist attacks certain vices in a woman such as the lust for money. He shows the evil effect of the excess of money in the case of a woman like Thea in *Augie March*. He also refers to Margaret who exploits money out of Tommy Wilhelm in a cruel manner. The nature of Margaret is known through the protagonist who happens to be her husband. Again, Sammler also refers to the physical vices of a woman when he remarks that a woman needs more washing, perfuming and so on. It appears that the novelist wants to bring about the physical and mental improvement of a woman. The woman in him is not a puppet. She has got a full personality of her own. If she occupies a subordinate place to man, it is only with a view to maintaining the unity of the family according to Jewish ideal. The approach of the novelist is moral and ethical. He proceeds to present the picture of a woman with certain moral perceptions in his mind.

Thus, from *Dangling Man* (1944) to *Ravelstein* (2000) Saul Bellow has given us a vast and rich gallery of living women of all kinds:

> His female characters are active, alive, creative and outspoken. They are shown, for the most part, as forging meaningful lives for themselves, struggling, working, searching, growing and achieving.[3]

Bellow has come a long way in his description of women characters. He has built a world of women which is mostly seen by men. It illuminates a whole region of the relationship between men and women.

Notes

1. Cronin, Gloria L. "An Introduction to Saul Bellow," *Saul Bellow Society and Journal*, Home Page.
2. *Ibid.*
3. Aharoni, Ada. 99-112.

Bibliography

A. PRIMARY SOURCES

(1) Books

Dangling Man, Penguin Books, 1987.

The Victim, Penguin Books, 1947.

The Adventures of Augie March, New York: Viking Press, 1953.

Seize the Day, Penguin Books, 1987.

Henderson the Rain King, New York: Viking Press, 1959.

Herzog, Penguin Books, 1976.

The Last Analysis (Play), New York: Viking Press, 1965.

Mosby's Memoirs and Other Stories, New York: Viking Press, 1968.

Mr. Sammler's Planet, Penguin Books, 1984.

Humboldt's Gift, New York: Viking Press, 1975.

To Jerusalem and Back, Harmondsworth: Penguin Books, 1977.

The Dean's December, New York: Harper and Row, 1982.

Him With His Foot in His Mouth and Other Stories, New York: Harper and Row, 1987.

More Die of Heartbreak, New York: William Morrow and Company, Inc., 1987.

A Theft, New York: Penguin Books, 1989.

The Bellarosa Connection, New York: Penguin Books, 1989.

The Actual, New York: Penguin Books, 1997.

Ravelstein, New York: Penguin Books, 2000.

(2) Articles, Reviews and Uncollected Short Works

"*A Personal Record,*" *New Republic,* 130 (February 22, 1954), 20.

"A Silver Dish," *The New Yorker,* September 25, 1978, 40-50, 55-56, 60.

"A Talk With the Yellow Kid," *The Reporter,* 15, September 6, 1956, 41-44.

"A Word From Writer Directly to Reader," *Fiction of the Fifties,* ed., Herbert Gold, New York, 1959.

"A Writer From Chicago," *The Tanner Lectures of Human Values*: III, ed. Steriling M. McMurrin. Salt Lake City: University of Utah Press, 1982.

"Culture Now: Some Animadversions, Some Laughs," *Modern Occasions,* 1, No. 2 (Winter 1971), 162-78.

"Deep Readers of the World, Beware!" *The New York Times Book Review,* February 15, 1959, 1, 34.

"Distractions of a Fiction Writer" *The Living Novel,* ed. Granville Hicks, New York, 1957, 1-20.

"Foreword," *The Closing of the American Mind,* New York: Simon and Schuster, 1987.

"Hemingway and the Image of Man," *Partisan Review,* 20 (May-June 1953), 338-42.

"How I Wrote Augie March's Story," *The New York Times Book Review,* January 31, 1954, 3, 17.

"Introduction," *Great Jewish Short Stories,* ed. Saul Bellow. New York: Dell, 1963, 3, 17.

"Machines and Story Books: Literature in the Age of Technology," *Harper's,* 249, August 1974, 48-59.

"Recent American Fiction," *Encounter,* 21 (November 1963), 22-29.

"Skepticism and the Depth of Life," *The Arts and the Public,* eds. James E. Miller and Paul D. Herring, Chicago: University of Chicago Press, 1967.

"The Jewish Writer and the English Literary Tradition," *Commentary,* 8, October, 1949, 366-67.

"Thinking Man's Wasteland" *Saturday Review,* April 3, 1965, 20.

"Two Morning Monologues", *Partisan Review,* 8 (May-June, 1947), 230-36.

"The Nobel Lecture," *The American Scholar,* 46, No. 3 (Summer 1977), 316-25.

"The Sealed Treasure" *The Open Forum,* ed. Alfred Kazin. New York, 1961, 3-9.

"The Swamp of Prosperity," *Commentary,* 38, July 1959, 77-79.

"The University as Villain," *Nation,* 185, November, 1957, 361-63.

"The Uses of Adversity," *The Reporter,* 21, October 1959, 42-44.

"The Writer as Moralist," *Atlantic,* 211, March 1963, 58-62.

"The Writer and the Audience," *Perspectives USA,* 9, Autumn 1954), 99-102.

"Where Do We Go From Here: The Future of Fiction," *Michigan Quarterly Review,* 1 (Winter 1962), 27-33.

(3) Interviews

Breit, Harvey, "Talk With Saul Bellow" *The New York Times Book Review,* 20 September, 1953, 22.

Enck, John, "Saul Bellow: An Interview." *Wisconsin Studies in Contemporary Literature,* 6 (1965), 156-60.

Kakutani, Michiko, "A Talk With Saul Bellow: On His Work and Himself." *The New York Times Book Review,* 13 December, 1981, 27-30.

Kulshrestha, Chirantan, "A Conversation with Saul Bellow," *Chicago Review,* 23, No. 4 and 24, No. 1, 7-15.

Roudane, Matthew C., "An Interview with Saul Bellow." *Contemporary Literature,* 25, No. 3 (Fall 1984), 265-280.

Singh, Sukhbir, Conversations with Saul Bellow. New Delhi: *Academic Foundation,* 1993.

_____, "Meeting with Saul Bellow," *American Studies International,* 35, No. 1 (February 1997), 19-31.

B. SECONDARY SOURCES

Abbot, H. Porter, "Saul Bellow and the 'Lost Cause' of Character," *Novel : A Forum On Fiction,* Vol. 13, 3 (Spring 1980): 264-83.

Aharoni, Ada, "Saul Bellow and Existentialism," *Saul Bellow's Newsletter,* 2, No. 2 (Spring-Summer 1983): 42-54.

_____, "Women in Saul Bellow's Novels," *Studies in American Jewish Literature* 3 (1983) 99-112.

Axelrod, Stephen Gould, "The Jewishness of Bellow's Henderson," *American Literature* 47 (November 1975): 439-43.

Bailey, Jennifer, "A Qualified Affirmation of Saul Bellow's Recent Work," *Journal of American Studies,* 7 (April 1973): 67-76.

Baumbach, Jonathan, "The Double Vision" The Victim, The Landscape of Nightmare, *Studies in the Contemporary American Novel,* New York: New York University Press, 1965, 35-54.

Belitt, Ben, "Saul Bellow: The Depth Factor", *Salmagundi* 30 (Summer 1975): 57-65.

Berets, Ralph, "Repudiation and Reality Instruction in Saul Bellow's Fiction," *Centennial Review* 20 (Winter 1976): 75-101.

Boyers, Robert, "Nature and Social Reality in Saul Bellow's Mr. Sammler's Planet," *Critical Quarterly* 15 (Autumn 1973): 34-56.

Braham, Jeanne, *A Sort of Columbus: The American Voyages of Saul Bellow's Fiction,* Athens: University of Georgia Press, 1984.

Bradbury, Malcolm, "Saul Bellow's Herzog," *Critical Quarterly,* 7 (Autumn 1965): 269-78.

Bradbury, Malcolm, "The It and the We: Saul Bellow's New Novel", *Encounter,* 45, No. 5 (November 1975): 61-67.

_____, *Saul Bellow,* Methuen London and New York, 1982.

Chavkin, Allan, "Bellow and English Romanticism," *Studies in the Literary Imagination,* 17, No. 2 (Fall 1984): 7-18.

_____, "The Problem of Suffering in Saul Bellow's Fiction", *Comparative Literature Studies,* 21, No. 2 (Summer 1984): 161-72.

Clayton, John J., *Saul Bellow: In Defence of Man,* Second Ed., Bloomington: Indiana University Press, 1971.

_____, Saul Bellow's *Seize the Day:* A Study in Mid Life Transition", *Saul Bellow Journal,* 5, No. 1 (Winter 1986), 34-42.

Cohen, Arthur A., *The Myth of the Judeo Christian Tradition,* New York: Schocken, 1971.

Cohen, Sarah Blacher, *Saul Bellow's Enigmatic Laughter,* Urbana: University of Illinois Press, 1974.

Cronin, Gloria L., "The Seduction of Tommy Wilhelm: A Post-Modernist Appraisal of *Seize the Day," Saul Bellow Journal,* 3, No. 1 (Fall/Winter 1983), 18-27.

_____, "*Henderson the Rain King*: A Parodic Expose of the Modern Novel," *Arizona Quarterly* 39, No. 3 (Autumn 1983): 266-76.

Cronin, Gloria L. and Goldman, L.H., *Saul Bellow in the 1980s: A Collection of Critical Essays*, Affiliated East-West Press, Pvt. Ltd., New Delhi, 1992.

Desai, Anita, "Bellow, the Rain King," *Salmagundi,* Spring-Summer, 1995, 63-65.

Dutton, Robert R., *Saul Bellow,* New York: Twayne, 1971.

Fiedler, Leslie A., "The Breakthrough: The American Jewish Novelist and the Fictional Image of the Jew," *Recent American Fiction Some Critical Views,* Boston, MA: Houghton-Mifflin, 1968.

Fuchs, Daniel, "Saul Bellow and the Modern Tradition," *Wisconsin Studies in Contemporary Literature,* 15 (Winter 1974): 67-89.

_____, "Bellow and Freud", *Studies in Literary Imagination* 17 No. 2 (1984): 59-80.

_____, *Vision and Revision,* Affiliated East-West Press Pvt. Ltd., New Delhi, 1992.

Galloway, David D., *Mr. Sammler's Planet*: Bellow's Failure of Nerve, *Modern Fiction Studies,* 19 (Spring 1973): 17-28.

Geismar, Maxwell, "Saul Bellow: Novelist of the Intellectuals", *American Moderns: From Rebellion to Conformity,* New York: Hill and Wang, 1958, 210-24.

_____, "The Jewish Heritage in Contemporary American Fiction," *Ramparts*, 2, No. 2 (Autumn 1963): 5-13.

Gold, Herbert, "Review of Henderson the Rain King," *Nation,* 188 (Feb. 21, 1989).

Goldman, L.H., *Saul Bellow's Moral Vision: A Critical Study of the Jewish Experience,* New York: Irvington Publishers, Inc. 1983.

_____, "Saul Bellow and the Philosophy of Judaism," *Studies in Literary Imagination* 17, No. 2 (1984): 81-95.

Harper, Howard M. "Saul Bellow—The Heart's Ultimate Need," *Desperate Faith,* Chapel Hill, North Coroline, 1967.

Harris, Mark, *Saul Bellow: Drumlin Woodchuck,* Athens: The University of Georgia Press, 1980.

Hopkinson, Tom, "Review of *Henderson the Rain King,*" *London Magazine* 1 (August 1954).

Kaplan, Harold, "The Second Fall of Man," *Salmagundi,* 30 (Summer 1975): 66-89.

King, Kathleen, "Bellow the Allegory King: Animal Imagery in *Henderson the Rain King,*" *Saul Bellow Journal,* 7, No. 1 (Winter 1988): 44-50.

Kristol, Irving, "Review of *Henderson the Rain King,*" *Encounter* 3 (July 1954).

Kulshrestha, Chirantan, *Saul Bellow: The Problem of Affirmation,* New Delhi: Arnold Heinemann, 1978.

Levine, Paul, "Saul Bellow: The Affirmation of the Philosophical Fool," *Perspectives,* 10 (Winter, 1959), 163-76.

Loe, Thomas, "Modern Allegory and the Form of *Seize the Day.*" *Saul Bellow Journal,* 7, No. 1 (Winter 1998): 57-66.

Malin, Irving, *Saul Bellow's Fiction,* Southern Illinois University Press, 1973.

Opdahl, Keith, *The Novels of Saul Bellow: An Introduction,* University Park: Pennsylvania State University Press, 1967.

_____, "Stillness in the Midst of Chaos: Plot in the Novels of Saul Bellow," *Modern Fiction Studies* 25 (Spring 1979): 15-28.

Pifer, Ellen, "Two Different Speeches: Mystery and Knowledge in *Mr. Sammler's Planet,*" *Mosaic,* 18, No. 2.

_____, "If the Shoe Fits: Bellow and Recent Critics," *Texas Studies in Language and Literature,* 29, No. 4 (Winter 1987): 442-57.

_____, *Saul Bellow: Against the Grain,* University of Pennysylvania Press, 1991.

Podhoretz, Norman, "Review of *Henderson the Rain King,*" *Commentary,* 16 (October 1953).

Porter, M. Gilbert, *Whence the Power? The Artistry and Humanity of Saul Bellow,* Columbia: University of Missouri Press, 1974.

Pritchett, V.S., "Review of *Henderson the Rain King,*" *New Statesman and Nation,* N.S. 47 (19 June, 1954).

Rovit, Earl, ed., *Saul Bellow: A Collection of Critical Essays,* Twentieth Century View, Englewood, Cliffs, N.J. Prentice Hall, 1975.

_____, "Saul Bellow and the Concept of the Survivor," *Saul Bellow and His Work,* ed. Edmond Schraepen, Brussels: Free University of Brussels, 1978.

Rodrigues, Eusebio L., "Saul Bellow's Henderson as America." *Centennial Review,* 20 (Spring 1976), 189-95.

Scheer Schazer, Briggitte, *Saul Bellow,* New York: Frederick Ungar, 1972.

Schraepen, Edmond, ed., *Saul Bellow and His Work,* Brussels: Free University of Brussels, 1978.

Schwartz, Delmore, "Review of *Dangling Man,*" *Partisan Review* (Summer 1944), 348-50.

Scott, Nathan A., "Bellow's Vision of the Axial Lines," *Three American Moralists : Mailer, Bellow, Trilling,* Bloomington: Indiana University Press, 1973.

Shaw, Peter, "The Tough Guy Intellectual," *Critical Quarterly,* 8 (Spring 1966) 13-28.

Siegel, Ben, "Artists and Opportunists in Saul Bellow's *Humboldt's Gift,*" *Wisconsin Studies in Contemporary Literature,* 3, No. 1 (Spring 1977), 20-25.

Simon, Elliot M., "Saul Bellow and the Scrament of Betrayal," *Yiddish,* 11, No. 3-4 (1999), 135-58.

Stevenson, David L., "Styron and the Fiction of the Fifties" *Critique* 3 (Summer 1960).

Stranger, James. "The Power of Vision: Blake's system and Bellow's Project in Mr. Sammler's Planet. *Saul Bellow Journal,* 12, No. 2 (Fall 1994): 17-36.

Tanner, Tony, *Saul Bellow,* New York: Oliver and Boyd, 1965.

_____, "Saul Bellow: The Flight from Monologue", *Encounter,* 24 (February 1965): 58-70.

Tanner, Stephen L., "The Religious Vision of *More Die of Heartbreak,*" Saul Bellow in the 1980's.

Tillich, Paul, *The Courage to Be,* New Haven: Yale University Press, 1952.

Trachtenberg, Stanley, "Saul Bellow's Luftmenschen: The Compromise with Reality," *Critique,* 9 No. 3 (1967): 37-61.

Trilling, Diana, *Reviewing the Forties,* New Yale: Harcourt Brace Jovanovich, 1978.

Trilling, Lionel, *The Opposing Self: Nine Essays in Criticism,* New York: The Viking Press, 1955.

Uphaus, Suzanne H., "From Innocence to Experience: A study of Herzog." *Dalhousie Review,* 46 (Spring 1966): 65-79.

Wheelis, Allen, *The Quest for Identity,* New York: W.W. Norton and Company, Inc., 1958.

Wilson Jonathan, *On Bellow's Planet: Readings from the Dark Side,* Rutherford, N.J. Fairleigh Dickinson University Press, 1985.

Walden, Daniel, "Saul Bellow's Paradox: Individualism and the Soul," *Saul Bellow Journal,* 12, No. 2 (Fall 1994): 58-71.

Weinberg, Helen, *The New Novel in America: The Kafkan Mode in Contemporary Fiction.* London: Cornell University Press, 1970.

Weinstein, Mark, "The Fundamental Elements in Mr. Sammler's Planet." *Saul Bellow Journal,* 1, No. 2 (Spring/Summer 1982): 18-26.

West, Ray B., Jr., "Six Authors in Search of a Hero", *Sewanee Review,* 65 (July-Sept. 1957): 498-08.